GUNS & THIGHS

Ram Gopal Varma is a film director, screenwriter and producer who has made films in Telugu and Hindi in a range of genres—psychological thrillers, gangster films, road movies, horror films and musicals. His first successful Hindi film was *Shiva*, but it was with *Rangeela*, which won Filmfare Awards for the lead actor and music director, that he truly gained recognition in Bollywood. His 'gangster trilogy', consisting of his masterpiece *Satya* along with *Company* and *Sarkar*, has garnered several Filmfare Awards, including a Critics Award for Best Film and a Best Director nomination. These films have been pioneers in their genre. The film *Shool*, that he produced, has won the National Award for Best Feature Film in Hindi. Ram Gopal Varma has also given breaks to many newcomers like Shimit Amin and Anurag Kashyap, who have gone on to become independent writers and film directors of note.

GUNS & THIGHS

THE STORY OF MY LIFE

RAM GOPAL VARMA

RUPA

Published by
Rupa Publications India Pvt. Ltd. 2016
7/16, Ansari Road, Daryaganj
New Delhi 110002

Sales centres:
Allahabad Bengaluru Chennai
Hyderabad Jaipur Kathmandu
Kolkata Mumbai

First published by hardcover in 2016
First published in Paperback in 2018

ISBN: 978-81-291-5110-0

First impression 2018

10 9 8 7 6 5 4 3 2 1

Owing to their tremendous contribution to my life in one way or the other, I dedicate this book to Mad *magazine, Ayn Rand, Urmila Matondkar, Bruce Lee, Amitabh Bachchan, porn star Tori Black and a few gangsters.*

Contents

Critics/The Media: Why I Love-Hate Them

Preface

'We live the life of others when we read their thoughts.'
—Ayn Rand

Many philosophers from Ayn Rand to Friedrich Nietzsche, fiction writers like James Hadley Chase and Frederick Forsyth and even humour magazines like *Mad* have made me live many lives, influenced me greatly and moulded my personality. They have also triggered many incidents and relationships which have shaped and steered my life. In my interviews and through my Twitter handle, I have always spoken my mind and delivered my opinions: loud, clear and uncensored. This book is another platform for explaining my ideas and the way I view the world, examining what motivated me to enter the film world, performing an honest post mortem on my films—the hits as well as the flops—and talking about some of the people who have shared my life—filmy and personal. I have never, ever since I've been old enough to have a mind of my own, believed in God, respected elders, valued friendships or cared for education. The one thing I have ardently relished, respected, valued, loved and trusted is film-making. I share some snippets from my filmy journey here with my readers. This book is a mere penning down of my thoughts, some of which might irritate you, some amuse you, some entertain you and some even make you hate me, but, at the end of the day, it won't stop me from speaking my mind and doing as I please. Irrespective of what anyone thinks of me, I will forever remain who I am—and if you think I'm bad and outrageous and terrible, I won't lose any sleep over it.

Friedrich Nietzsche said, 'There are no facts, only interpretations.' It follows that more than what I meant, what's important is what you make of this book.

Ram Gopal Varma

EVERYBODY IS A NOBODY:
SUCCESS IS CHANCE

Chapter 1

Everybody is a Nobody

I HAVE OFTEN BEEN credited with discovering talent and giving many actors and technical people breaks. But the plain truth is that I gave them their breaks, not because I divined some great genius in them and could foresee future acclaim for them. Quite honestly, I never thought anything of anybody. The reason I took Anurag Kashyap in *Satya* had nothing to do with my perception of his talent, but it was because he was the first writer to approach me after I decided to make the film. And later on, he got Saurabh Shukla to join as a co-writer. Why I credited Saurabh Shukla ahead of Anurag in the titles of *Satya* was because he was older in age than Anurag.

People thought Anurag was the main guy of the two because I continued to work with Anurag and not Saurabh.

The reason I did so was because Saurabh got married and he did not have as much time as Anurag to hang out with me.

Similarly, I did not think that Shimit Amin of *Ab Tak Chappan* was more talented than Prawaal Raman of *Gayab* just because *Ab Tak Chappan* was a hit and *Gayab* a flop. On the contrary, I believe that given the material of *Ab Tak Chappan*, Prawaal would have made a better film and given the material of *Gayab*, Shimit might have come up with a worse film. But that's just my opinion and it's not necessarily true.

I made *Satya* and *Daud* back-to-back. So who is the real me? Anurag made *No Smoking* and *Dev D*...so who is the real Anurag?

Likewise, why would Rakeysh Omprakash Mehra make a flop like *Aks* first and a masterpiece like *Rang De Basanti* next? Why did Ashutosh Gowariker waste his time and talent on *Baazi* if he could make a *Lagaan*?

The fact is that each and every one of us is as good or as bad as the material we take up at that particular time, and how things fall in place after that. Fair enough, the material I or anyone else picks up is an individual choice, but without knowing what factors affected that choice at that particular time, one cannot take it for granted that someone is either very talented or has lost it.

In effect, I am saying that if Anurag had come to me for *Daud*, we would have ended up making as bad a film and if

Sanjay Chhel who wrote *Daud* had written *Satya,* it would have turned out as good. Incidentally, Sanjay Chhel also wrote *Rangeela.* I am not taking away the credit from Anurag or Saurabh, or the various actors and technicians of *Satya.* All I am saying is that we all shone in *Satya* because of the material I picked up by chance, and 'chance' is the operative word here. If I knew unerringly what material to pick up, why would I also be making bad films?

In a good film, everything just falls in place. Everyone connected with it should just be happy it's panned out so and not believe themselves to be the architects of its success. They should feel thankful that nobody realizes that a good film or a bad film happens just by chance.

What I tell young filmmakers is that 'the day you start thinking that the film is only you, that is when you start taking yourself too seriously and falling in love with the "I" and losing track of the source of the "I". In other words, it spells hubris.'

If I come up with a hundred ideas, ten could be film ideas and ninety could be other ideas and many a time they fail too. But people only know of my failed films because they are in the spotlight.

For instance, my video library business from the perspective of my family and my colleagues in the video business was considered a huge success at that time. Only I know it was a big flop and here's why.

The reason I started the video library was that I knew around twenty of my friends and relatives owned video players. So I thought that if between them they hired twenty cassettes, at ₹10 a cassette a day, I would get ₹200 a day or ₹6,000 a month, which was the running cost of my shop. Anything extra, I thought, would be a profit which I could take a chance upon. Within a month of starting my shop, I was renting out more than 100 cassettes a day, but none of the twenty people I had counted upon ever came to my shop. If they did, they never paid, as they were my friends or were related to me. So in effect, what I had counted upon didn't happen and success came from unexpected quarters. But I know in my heart that if I had not banked on those twenty people, there was no way I would have started my shop.

So am I a success or a failure? I would say that I am a failure in terms of intent and successful by chance. I believed in *Raat* more than in *Shiva*, and only made *Shiva* first because the producers wouldn't let me make *Raat*. I believed in *Daud* more than *Rangeela* and the proof of that is, why would I make a film like *Daud* after *Rangeela* unless I thought it was better?

I believed in all my leading actors from Nagarjuna Akkineni to J. D. Chakravarthi, Manoj Bajpayee and Vivek Oberoi. I believed in Urmila, Antara, Nisha, and Anaika to the same extent, and in Anurag Kashyap, Jaideep Sahani, Sajid-Farhad and Prashant Pandey; and despite the ups and downs of their career graphs, my belief in all of them remains unshaken.

Anyway, the point I'm trying to make is that all my successes were by default and all my failures were by intent.

Then what has made me carry on for so long? It is nothing but the ability to keep on making decisions. A decision led to my making an appalling film like *Daud* after the super success of *Rangeela*, and a decision led to my making a highly experimental film with sweaty bearded faces like *Satya* after the failure of the much-hyped *Daud*.

I would any day go on deciding to make good, bad and ugly films rather than sit in a coffee shop, having endless cups of coffee, tearing down others' films and planning a masterpiece in the future, which might never go on the floors.

To those critics who complain that I make films in a hurry, my answer is that I would rather live in the moment and make my film right now, than endlessly plan in the hope of it becoming a masterpiece. Incidentally, the longest time I have taken and maximum money I have spent in my career are on three films—*Daud, Aag* and *Department*—which are three of my biggest flops.

I rest my case.

Chapter 2

Dustbin Fortunes

Cycle 1

WHEN I WAS TRYING to get a break, I used to attend the music composing sessions of a film which was being made by director B. Gopal at the time. In the course of those sessions, whenever its music director Chakravarti and director B. Gopal used to go for lunch, I used to chat with the music director's assistant and once in a while he used to hum tunes which he had himself composed. I was very impressed with many of his tunes. One day, I described to him a scene from the script of *Shiva* and the way I intended to shoot it, and asked him what kind of music he thought there should be in the scene.

He replied that there should be none. I was mighty impressed with the answer, and committed to him that if ever I got a break, I would sign him on as my music director.

Finally, when I got the break I suddenly had the opportunity of signing on Ilayaraja. Feeling very guilty, I told the assistant music director that I wouldn't be taking him for the film as I was getting Ilayaraja. He was obviously very heartbroken, but said that he understood the situation and wished me all the best. But because of the time I had spent with him and the association I had developed, the guilt was killing me and the moment *Shiva* became a big hit, I went back to him and signed him up for my second film. The assistant's name was Keeravani (also known as M.M. Kreem) and the film I signed him on for was my second telugu film *Kshana Kshanam*. Of all the films I've made till date, I consider *Rangeela* and *Kshana Kshanam* the two with the best musical scores.

A keyboard player used to be working for Keeravani and I used to interact with him a lot, especially when he was doing the background soundtracks and I always believed that he could become a very good music director if he tried. He, however, didn't want to, saying that he was technically not a composer. Much later, when I had a problem with R.D. Burman during *Drohi (Antham)* and I could not get Keeravani as he was busy, I forced that keyboard player to do one song.

Both the song and the film didn't work, but later on when

a film with megastar Chiranjeevi came up, I told Chiranjeevi that the *Drohi* song hadn't worked but I really believed in the keyboard player's potential as a music composer. Chiranjeevi said that if he was good enough for me, he was good enough for him. The keyboard player was ecstatic, but after a great celebratory launch, the Chiranjeevi film was shelved for a variety of reasons and the poor guy was devastated. However, on the strength of the impression he made on Chiranjeevi through a song he recorded for the shelved film, he was given another film by the latter, called *Choodalani Vundi*, which set him firmly on the path to becoming one of the top music composers in the Telugu film industry. The keyboard player's name is Mani Sharma.

Cycle II

When my first film *Shiva* was ready for background score, there was a musicians union strike in Chennai, and so Ilayaraja and I shifted to Mumbai to record the score. The musical team chosen by Ilayaraja in Mumbai saw the film, and one particular violin player walked up to me and said that the film would create a sensation. Technically that was the first compliment I had ever received from an outsider in my career. After that, the violin player and I would chat once in a while in the period the background score was being recorded.

A few years later, I signed R. D. Burman for *Drohi* and went to Mumbai for recording a song. Those days I used to operate from Hyderabad and kept flying up and down to Mumbai. I again bumped into the violin player. After telling me how happy he was at *Shiva's* success, which he had predicted, he brought a guy and introduced him as his closest friend and told me that he was a lyricist. That guy gave me a visiting card. I put the card in my pocket, and in the evening I returned to Hyderabad and forgot all about it.

Like I mentioned earlier, as I fell out with R. D. Burman for various reasons, I had to record a song with a new music director. As I was leaving for Chennai in the evening, my mom brought in a bunch of visiting cards collected over a period of time to ask me if she could throw them away. I quickly glanced through them and just kind of registered the card which the lyricist had given me before telling her to throw the lot away.

By the time I landed in Chennai, I got news that Javed Akhtar who was supposed to come with the lyrics to Chennai was not coming as he was stuck with some work. I got cheesed off and asked my guys in Mumbai to send a lyricist that night itself as I didn't want to cancel the recording. I was told that none was available. I suddenly remembered the visiting cards my mother had shown me. So I called her up and asked her, and she said that she already thrown them in the dustbin. She rummaged in the bin and luckily found the lyricist's card and gave me the number. I immediately got that lyricist flown to Chennai and he wrote the song for *Drohi*, and it was composed by Mani Sharma and recorded.

Both *Drohi* and the song bombed but my relationship with the lyricist continued, and whenever I was in Mumbai, the violin player, lyricist and I used to meet up once in a while. At that time I was just beginning to work on the idea of *Rangeela*. When I mentioned the story to both of them, they got very excited and the violin player composed a tune for which the lyricist wrote a song. I was very impressed and committed to both of them that they would be doing the music for *Rangeela*. They were thrilled to bits.

A few days later, Mani Ratnam made me hear the songs of *Roja* at his home in Chennai, and I was simply blown away with the orchestral brilliance of A. R. Rahman. I became greedy to have that sound in my film at any cost, and went back on my commitment to the violin player and signed on Rahman instead, which understandably left the violin player very angry and heartbroken. The lyricist pleaded with me not to renege on my promise to his friend, but I said it was a professional decision in the best interest of the film.

I spoke to Rahman about the lyricist and told him that his first song hadn't worked, but I believed he was very good. Rahman said, 'If he is good enough for you he is good enough for me.'

Thus Mehboob came into *Rangeela* minus the violin player, and the first song he wrote was '*Tanha Tanha*'. I played that song to Mani Ratnam and he was mighty impressed with the fact that it was the first song he'd heard in a long time which didn't have the words 'dil', 'deewana' and 'sanam', and he signed on Mehboob for *Bombay*.

With the super success of both *Bombay* and *Rangeela*, Mehboob became a very big name, and then he recommended his closest friend—the violin player—to Sanjay Leela Bhansali, who was looking for a new music director for *Hum Dil De Chuke Sanam*, and thus was born Ismail Darbar.

After the tremendous musical success of *Hum Dil De Chuke Sanam*, which also coincided with a couple of Rahman albums, including my own *Daud*, not doing well, Ismail Darbar was hailed as the new musical kid on the block. I called him up to congratulate him but he didn't answer my calls.

Later on, Ismail gave an interview where he said that now that he was a success, everybody was calling him including Ram Gopal Varma. That was obviously his revenge for the heartache I gave him by dumping him for Rahman.

The close friends Ismail and Mehboob, who were responsible for the success of each other's career, broke up after *Devdas* because of differences which they didn't spell out in public and both went into a decline professionally after that. Now, when they sometimes try to call me to patch up and bury the hatchet, I don't pick up the calls of either as I have moved on to a new set of people and don't have either the time or the inclination to dwell on old relationships.

Anyway, the whole point is that I am just so fascinated with how the cycle of fortune keeps on throwing people in and out of dustbins.

Chapter 3

Awards Are Bull

AS FAR AS I'M concerned, the only value awards have is the entertainment the gala ceremonies held to confer them provide. On the negative side, they can be corrupting, not necessarily in terms of who is given what award, but their very structure itself. To start with, filmmaking is a team effort and the director is the only person to judge the contribution of the team members, as their work is being benchmarked against his vision and requirements. It's possible that the director screws up fantastic work by a very capable technician by using it in the wrong context, and it's equally possible that bad work by an average technician is easily covered up by the overall effect. In both cases, it is the director's vision and skill that make or break the work done by other team members.

I find it strange that for all the euphoria generated amongst Indians by Resul Pookutty winning an Oscar, it did not even occur to them to ask what he has done before. He must have worked in fifty-odd films before *Slumdog Millionaire* and they would have ranged from the good, to the bad and ugly but the point is that his sound designing in them went unnoticed. With the media screaming about his great achievement, everybody was suddenly talking about his great talent. Did anybody think to ask or care, let alone know, who had got the same award the year before or after Resul? Does anybody even know, for that matter, what sound designing is?

I have never heard of or met a single person who saw *Slumdog* and singled out sound in particular, until the time Resul got an award; and from then on everybody talked knowledgably about sound design without having the faintest idea what it means.

A film has a live effects track, a dialogue track, an atmospheric track and the background score track, of which the sound designer is responsible for only a part. All of these are made to come together by the final mixing engineer to create the desired effect, sometimes in consultation with the director and sometimes without. Anybody hearing the mixed track has no way of knowing who is responsible and to what degree for the final effect. The only person who would know is the mixing engineer—and possibly the director—who decides what to keep, what to throw out and the sound levels.

I'm not trying to undermine Resul's work here, but to point out that better work by Resul may go unnoticed while something more average can create an impact for reasons unrelated to his work.

Coming to actors' performances, if the comparison, for instance, is between Aamir Khan for X role, Abhishek Bachchan for Y role and Shah Rukh Khan for Z role, my question is, how can anyone know whether SRK playing Y role would have done a better job than Abhishek or not; or whether Aamir in Z role would have been better than SRK or not? What I'm asking is, are they giving awards to actors or characters? If it's characters, then they are written by writers and how that character translates on screen is dependent on a number of factors such as screenplay, co-actors' performances, editing and direction, and there is no justification for the actor alone being given the credit. Unlike the stage, the only true judgment of cinematic acting can be done between the start and cut of a shot. It is because it is only here that the actor alone is drawing up an emotion on cue and releasing it, and thus, is solely responsible for his performance. So, how well he has matched the character to the director's vision, only the director can know; and then it's also possible that even a great performance can be completely screwed up by the director on the editing table, or if it is wrongly placed in the screenplay, or by an ineffective performance by a co-actor. So, a number of people's talents and their complex interweaving pool together in the sum total effect of a film moment or the film itself; and there is no way an outside body, irrespective of its expertise, can judge the individual contributions.

I have always maintained that my successful films owe to team effort and my failures are mine alone. The reason for that is that each and every actor and technician is contributing his work and talent as per my vision, and in many cases delivering far beyond my expectations. If I use their contributions wrongly, the film does not work. But when it works and I am being praised, I know in my heart which individuals specifically lifted a particular moment in the film or the film in its entirety even.

So in short, the success of a film is due to the contribution of the actors and technicians in excess of my expectations, which is why it belongs to them, while failure belongs to me alone, as it means that I failed in channelizing their equally great contributions to their intended destination.

It has to be realized that in the making of a film the technicians and actors are working towards satisfying the director, and the director is working towards satisfying the audience. So I find the concept of an outside body giving awards ridiculous, knowing as I do the mechanics of making a film.

Chapter 4

Chitti's Bar

THE YEAR I MADE *Raat,* which bombed badly, a cousin of mine called Chitti decided to open a bar and restaurant on Mehdipatnam Road in Hyderabad. He reckoned that with an investment of just ₹20 lakh, he could make a crore in the very first year. There was a huge colony on that road and not a single bar within 5 km either way of the location he had chosen. His logic seemed infallible and I wished him all the very best. By the end of the year, he had lost his investment and closed down the bar for lack of business. Then, he sadly figured that none of the residents of the colony wanted to drink in a bar in the vicinity of their homes and that's why nobody had ever opened a bar there in the first place.

Whether his reasoning was correct or not, the fact was that

both *Raat* and Chitti's Bar flopped, with one major difference. Since I am part of the film industry, everyone got to know about my failure but no one except me knew about Chitti's.

In the run-up to the Iraq war there was a lot of opposition to America attacking Iraq, including among Americans. They all questioned the authenticity of the information about Saddam Hussein stockpiling weapons of mass destruction, and said that innocent women and children would die in the war. But nobody ever doubted that America would be able to conquer Iraq.

After the attack, the war was over in a week. Saddam and his sons went into hiding, and the US President gave a speech with a banner screaming 'Mission accomplished' in the backdrop. But for years after that, the US did not know how to get out of Iraq without making things worse than before. If less than 200 Americans died in the war before they overthrew Saddam's regime, more than 12,000 Americans died after that in insurgent operations.

The interesting point here is that I don't remember either the American state or a single opponent of the war, including statesmen and common people, predicting this post-war scenario. But now, after the fact, every street-corner paanwala sniggers at America's flop show. I call it 'America ki Aag'.

Coming to films, over the years so many people ask me in surprise how I could have made such-and-such a flop. What they don't realize is that a film is made on the basis of a series of decisions taken over a long period of time, each relevant in a particular context.

There are a hell of a lot of things which can go wrong between the intent and execution of a film. Also how the film is eventually perceived by others, namely the audience, might be very different from the filmmaker's vision. This is because the audience views it maybe in a different time and context from that in which the idea was conceived by the filmmaker.

I have always maintained that all my flops are by intent and all my hits are by accident. That is because any of us will act upon anything if, and only if, we are convinced about something but what comes of our action is rarely under our control.

I know of a friend who was dating this girl for seven years and when they finally got married, their marriage was a big flop. When I asked him why, he said that they had both discovered some things about each other which they had never known in the seven years of dating.

The point I am trying to make is that apart from films, lots of things in our lives flop regularly, because a flop is nothing but a decision gone wrong. We are all experts at criticizing and commenting on others' failures, but very rarely are we experts at predicting and dissecting our own failures.

Mahesh Bhatt said that Sunil Gavaskar once told him that if he failed in a match, after coming back to the pavilion, even the attendant removing his knee pads would tell him how he should not have hit so-and-so ball. It is another matter that the attendant might not even have known how to hold a bat, but he would feel free to advise and give gyan to Gavaskar since he had flopped.

Coming back to Chitti, believing in his reasons, his family backed him financially. If the bar had become a hit, he would have been hailed as a visionary but since it flopped, he is now considered blindly stupid by his family because it could not afford the loss he made it undergo. In the case of my video library business, on the other hand, my family thought I was being blindly stupid and hence did not support me financially, but I became a visionary once the video library became a hit. But why I thought the library would be successful was not why it worked, whereas why Chitti thought the bar would be successful was the very reason it failed. So we both failed in what we intended but I succeeded by accident.

Chapter 5

You're Only as Good as Your Last Film

BASU CHATTERJEE WAS ONCE a name to reckon with. In the era of commercial formula films like *Deewaar* and *Zanjeer*, he successfully went against the grain to make cult films like *Rajnigandha, Chhoti Si Baat* and *Chitchor*. I remember seeing *Chitchor* seven times somewhere in the late 1970s or early 1980s, and the simplicity of narration that I learnt from it was pretty much what shaped my vision of *Rangeela*.

Cut to twenty years later

I was at my office in Mumbai, when my receptionist called me and said that someone called Basu Chatterjee had come to meet me. I asked the receptionist, 'Who is he?' and he said, 'He claims that he is a director. ' I got a shock and wondered why he had come. I walked to the reception to see a gentle-looking elderly man and welcomed him into my room.

I offered him coffee and started telling him how I used to stand in line outside Ramakrishna theatre in Hyderabad to watch his films. He smiled and told me that he was aware of it, as I had mentioned it many a time in my interviews over the years.

After a chat, he finally told me why he had come. Apparently, he had a script and a producer but he did not have access to any actors. He was desperately trying to get in touch with Manoj Bajpayee, but was unable to do so. So he had come to seek my help in accessing Manoj.

I said 'Sure', went into the other room and called Manoj. His phone was switched off, so I called his secretary. The secretary told me Manoj was out of town, and when I asked him if they knew that Basu Chatterjee was trying to get in touch he said, 'Yeah, I am figuring out how to get rid of him.'

I was pretty taken aback. I realized that while Manoj couldn't have been capable of such abruptness, he, for whatever reason, was not interested in working with Basu Chatterjee.

I came back and told Basuji, 'Manoj is not in town, so I will talk to him and get back.' He chatted for some more time and left.

Then a few days later Basuji called me and said, 'Apparently Manoj is back in town, but I have a feeling he doesn't want to work with me.' I didn't know what to say to that. Then he asked if I could recommend to Aftab Shivdasani that he listen to his—Basuji's—story. I said I would and after hanging up called Aftab and said, 'Aftab, Basu Chatterjee wants to meet you.' He said, 'Sure, sir, but who is he?'

Considering that Aftab is perhaps two generations removed from Basu Chatterjee, that answer didn't shock me. So I explained to him that Basuji was a highly successful director who had made cult films like *Chitchor*. Aftab asked, 'But sir, what does he do now?' I told Aftab, 'Look here, I don't know what he's been doing recently or what he is going to do now but being such a respected senior director the least you can do is to meet him and hear his story.' Aftab said, 'Ok sir, please give him my number. With a sigh of relief, I gave Aftab's number to Basuji and got back to my work.

Two days later, I got a call from Basuji thanking me. I asked him if Aftab had come to meet him. He said, 'No, he didn't have time so he sent his secretary to hear the story.' I didn't know what to say to that. So after a long pause I asked, 'So did his secretary listen to the story?' He said, 'No, the secretary after listening for ten minutes, said he had to rush somewhere. So I couldn't finish it. Anyway thanks for whatever you tried to do for me,' and hung up.

That's the last I heard of Basu Chatterjee. It was sometime in 2000, and for the last fifteen years, I haven't even heard his name mentioned. What remains is a faintly uncomfortable memory of my 'respectful' interaction with him.

Chapter 6

Hits and Flops

I BELIEVE THAT HITS and flops are meaningless emotional terms. I say this because a film in a true sense is a one-on-one experience between the filmmaker and each individual viewer. A film is made because the filmmaker has a story, which he desires to tell, and film business is about carrying the film effectively to as many viewers as possible and in the process making money out of it. There is the hardware of the film business, which is the hundreds of theatres in existence and hundreds still being built across the country, and they need software to play.

And then there are the thousands of people cinema gives a livelihood to—actors, technicians, producers, distributors, suppliers—and that's why it's called an industry. Now the industry needs to fill the theatres to run the business and it doesn't care as much about the quality of the film as about the turnover. Quality is important only from the filmmaker's perspective and the individual viewer's perspective, as it is very subjective because each individual has very specific taste, sensibility and intelligence.

We keep hearing that 90 per cent of films are flops, and nobody even thinks of asking how any industry can run if it is losing money 90 per cent of the time. This is how it happens. Let's say a producer spends ₹10 crore in making a movie which goes in payments to various artistes, technicians, suppliers, etc. Then let's say somebody buys it for ₹12 crore. The buyer further retails it to various others for, say, a sum total of ₹13 crore and the film finally collects ₹15 crore. Now this would be a case of the film making money for everyone involved. Let's say now the producer spent ₹16 crore, but the film was bought for only ₹12 crore because the sale price never depends on the cost price. It depends on the producer's compulsion to sell in order to safeguard himself and the buyer's perception of its value for the consumer. In the above case, it is a flop for the producer, but for the buyer it is a hit. This is the financial part of it. Coming to the creative part, *Darr* is a superhit for Shah Rukh and a super flop for Sunny Deol as far as their star branding is concerned.

In the year *Satya* was released, a Salman Khan starrer

called *Bandhan*, directed by K. Murli Mohan Rao, was released around the same time, and collected much more than *Satya*. But was it because the audience genuinely liked it better than *Satya*, or was it because Salman is a crowd puller? The fact that a film has good collections does not necessarily mean people liked it more than films that collected less. It only means that more people saw it. For instance, *Satya* was taken off from the theatres on the second or third day in parts of UP and Rajasthan for lack of audience. So it registered a super flop in those areas. But a year later, when I went to those areas for some other work, everybody recognized me as the director of *Satya*. How did that happen? It was simply because when it was released, nobody had heard about it and did not go to see it. By the time they heard about it, it was taken off from the theatres. So they must have finally seen it on video or cable. Today I doubt that you'll find a single individual who will say that he liked *Bandhan* more than *Satya*, but the collections at that time told a different story.

Now coming to the individual viewer's point of view, I will try to explain it with the help of an example. Suppose you go to a crockery store to buy a dinner set. You will check out the various designs available and pick the one you like best. You will never ask the salesman if it's a hit or flop, and neither will you ask a critic to review it. Anyone with a mind of his own will do the same with a movie.

Often you will hear about a film's opening in terms of percentage. Let's say a film opens in ten theatres, each with a 200-seat capacity. On the first screening, if all shows are full, it will register as 100 per cent opening, meaning 2,000 people saw it. But if the distributor opens it in twenty theatres and it registers 50 per cent opening, it is considered below the mark; but the bottom line is that 2,000 people still saw it. Undoubtedly, the additional theatres will incur extra theatre rentals and print costs, but that decision will always be with the distributor of the concerned circuit based on his perception and vision of how many people will watch it and has nothing to do with the filmmaker. But eventually, it is the filmmaker's branding which will suffer on account of ignorance and a bad decision made by someone else.

To sum it up strictly from a filmmaker's perspective, I would define a film as a hit or a flop going by what the film cost the producer to make, and how much he could recover on first sale. Any further trading of it is strictly dependent on various people's decisions about how to and how not to market it, which cannot be controlled by the filmmaker unless he is also a producer and a distributor.

If a wholesaler or retailer tries to sell an Ayn Rand book to a Mills and Boon-reading public, he is bound to be unsuccessful. And I don't think Ayn Rand could really be blamed for the failure. Going by his worldview, a filmmaker will make a film which some will love, some hate and some ridicule on an individual level, which is perfectly alright. What is not so straightforward is that the filmmaker's and actors' branding will also suffer on account of decisions about print deployment, occupancy percentages, box-office figures, etc. But I guess that's a professional hazard.

Chapter 7

Heroes' Guns and Heroines' Thighs

I WAS OBSESSED WITH films and everything in them. Be it the gun in Amitabh Bachchan's hands in *Zanjeer* or Sridevi's thighs in *Himmatwala*...everything about films used to give me almost orgasmic pleasure.

Even after finishing my civil engineering, getting married and managing a job as a site engineer, my obsession didn't die; on the contrary it reached fever pitch. My father was a sound engineer in Annapurna Studios in Hyderabad, and owing to that had reasonable access to the big guns there. One fine day, when my film mania reached its absolute peak, I went to him and declared that I wanted to be a film director. He looked at me as if I were stark raving mad, and with good reason, because there was not a single constructive thing that I had done in my life until then. I was a bad student and had the reputation of being a useless bum.

Realizing that he wasn't going to help, I started trying other means. A few years before I decided to try my hand at film direction, Andhra Pradesh's biggest newspaper magnate Ramoji Rao, had started a production house which had made quite a fresh bunch of non-run-of-the-mill films like *Pratighatana* and *Srivaariki Premalekha*. In order to somehow obtain access to him, I wrote an article for his now-defunct newspaper *Newstime,* titled 'The Ideas that Killed 30 Million People'. The editor was startled by the title, but after reading it he agreed to publish it.

Soon, on the strength of being the author of that article, I managed an appointment with Ramoji Rao and pitched my idea of directing a film for him. He rejected my pitch outright on the grounds of my lack of practical experience. I argued that a director does not need experience, only clarity of vision and the skill to communicate it to the actors and technicians. He did not buy it.

I was completely disillusioned with the experience, as he was the only option I had. My salary as a site engineer was just ₹800 per month and it was damn difficult to make ends meet. My wife Ratna was really worried about her future with a guy as impractical as me, and she requested her father to get me a job in Nigeria. He managed to get me a job paying ₹4,000 per month, which was obviously a huge jump from the ₹800 and very much needed by my family.

The 1-kilometre walk

I gave up the idea of being a director, and began preparing to go to Nigeria. One of the documents necessary for the purpose was an international driving licence. A friend of mine called Naidu was taking me on his bike to an RTO office, where he knew someone who would do the needful. En route he stopped at a video library called Priyadarshini Videos owned by his friend. Those were the days when video libraries were just coming up, and that was the first time I had ever been inside one. As Naidu was chatting with his friend, I was checking out the cassettes and suddenly had the brainwave of starting a video library myself. With my extensive knowledge about films, I was confident of making a go of it. By evening I had become so obsessed with the idea that I took my father's scooter and went all over town to check out six or seven video libraries, and by night I had firmly made up my mind to drop the idea of going to Nigeria. I decided that I would make a film myself with the profits I earned from the library. Everyone including my father, grandfather and Ratna thought I had completely lost it, and Ratna understandably was in tears.

I didn't have any money at all for my business enterprise. So I went about asking for loans varying from ₹1,000 to ₹3,000 and managed to raise about ₹20,000 from some eight people. That was just enough for buying cassettes, but not for renting a shop. My father was nearing retirement and he was pretty worried about how to run the house. One of my uncles had a shop in Ameerpet area, which he had given to my father without taking a deposit. My father was planning to start a juice parlour there as a retirement plan. I went to him and asked him for the shop for my video library. He just kept quiet and I thought he wanted some time to think about it and left him.

The following night, my uncle took me to a bar and while having a drink told me how distressed my father was with my asking for the shop. My father had apparently told him that what he had kept for his old age was also being demanded from him. I was so upset with this that I decided to drop the video library idea, return the loans I had taken and resume my preparations for Nigeria. Now, the bar where my uncle broke the news was a kilometre away from my house. I started walking with tears in my eyes, meaning to go and tell my father that he could have his shop back. But as I walked, my emotions slowly started subsiding and logic started exerting itself.

I told myself that just because my father was feeling disturbed was not reason enough for me to give up on a plan I believed would work, financially and in every other way. So the choice was between making him momentarily unhappy with prospects of long-term happiness, and making him happy for the present with all of us remaining unhappy for the rest of our lives. Logic prevailed by the time I finished the 1-kilometre walk, and I just ignored my father and went about my preparations of setting up the video library.

The video library was a huge success and started earning more than ₹20,000 a month, which was a massive jump over my salary of ₹800 per month and my dad's of ₹1,500. My father had never smiled so brightly before, and to this day I can't forget the pride with which he looked at me. Also, this sudden change in my financial status gave me the confidence to try again for a break in films.

The point I want to make is that the primary reason for my becoming a director was the unscheduled stop Naidu made at the video library, and that 1-kilometre distance between the bar and my house which allowed me the time required for my logic to win over my emotions.

Chapter 8

Wrong is Right

IN *SARKAR* SELVAR MANI says, '*Jiske paas power hai uska wrong bhi right ho jata hai.*' I believe it's not so much power alone, but also your attitude towards life. Whenever life decides something for me, I immediately decide to use the turn of events in a certain way so that I always manage to come out on top.

When I decided to start a video library with a capital of ₹20,000, I went about trying to buy quality video films. In the process, I trusted a friend's father who sold me faulty tapes worth ₹10,000, which either didn't play or got stuck in the video players, thereby reducing my capital to half even before I started. So by the time I started my shop, I barely had a 100 workable tapes. My shop, which I called Movie House, was located in Ameerpet and everyone told me that it was a very bad idea to start a shop there as it had a predominantly lower-middle/middle class population that could not afford video cassette recorders (VCR). I was also told that my shop couldn't compete with a library called Fantasy on Punjagutta Road as the rich Banjara Hills crowd only patronized that library. Once it started, my library became successful within a month and Fantasy soon went out of business. Now the same people said that these days everybody owned a VCR, and that Movie House had better parking space than Fantasy.

If something doesn't work, people will say 'we told you so', and if it works, they will come up with a new theory and will conveniently forget what they had said earlier. For my films, as for my video library, I get a lot of unsolicited advice. I was told *Daud* would be a blockbuster because it had Sanjay Dutt after *Khal Nayak*, and Urmila and Rahman after *Rangeela*, and I was advised to shelve *Satya* because nobody wanted to see sweaty-looking faces in dirty locations.

The same people advised me not to do *Aag* and my various other failures, and today they will all remember what they said about *Aag* and conveniently forget what they said about *Satya*. It's not that things turned out the way I'd envisaged either. In starting my video shop, apart from trusting my friend's father, I placed my trust in about twenty people I knew who had VCRs, who I was sure would give me business. The business grew to 100 cassettes per day but those twenty never came and if some did, they didn't pay on account of their closeness to me.

So eventually, neither was I correct in what I believed, nor were my various well-wishers. Random things keep happening, which are completely out of your control, and you can only control your reaction to an out-of-control situation. My real success, I believe, lies in my ability to make decisions and implement them superfast.

Anyway, coming back to the video library, I used to narrate the stories of the films to my customers depending on their tastes. In due course of time, they became so addicted to my story sessions, many said my narration was better than the films.

So I sat behind the counter of the shop for about eight months doing fantastic business, and with just the one high point of being arrested and put into Punjagutta Police station lock-up for pirating Amitabh Bachchan's *Aakhree Raasta.* That was my first close encounter with the police and I made friends with them and studied their psychology, and later put that understanding to good use in my cop films. Incidentally, Movie House, which I gave up when I started shooting *Shiva,* has been replaced by Rajdoot Sweet Home.

Coming back to 'wrong is right', one day I overheard my father telling someone that Venkat, the brother of Nagarjuna, was looking for a story for a film, as he had K. Raghavendra Rao (of *Himmatwala* fame) signed up. Venkat's brother-in-law,

Surendra, was a customer at my shop and through him I managed to get an appointment with Venkat. I told him the story of *Raatri* (*Raat*) which he said wouldn't work in the Telugu market. He asked me if I could write a story for a hero to be told to Raghavendra Rao. So I went back and in about an hour, wrote a one-line order of *Shiva,* based on my own experiences in college and borrowing liberally from Govind Nihalani's *Ardh Satya*, Rahul Rawail's *Arjun* and Dilip Shankar's *Kaal Chakra*.

Venkat liked the story very much and took me to narrate it to Raghavendra Rao. Mr Rao that said it sounded like an experimental film and had no drama in it. I thought maybe he knew what he was talking about since he was so successful and asked him if I could work on it. As I was trying to rework it, I happened to see his film *Kaliyuga Pandavulu,* and I suddenly realized how he must be seeing *Shiva*. I immediately gave up the idea of being a story writer and went and told Venkat. I asked him if there was any director I could assist, as everyone felt that was a very important precondition to my becoming a director. Surendra, to whom I had become quite close by then, was starting a film with director B. Gopal called *Collectorgari Abbayi* starring Nagarjuna and his dad Akkineni Nageshwara Rao. So I formally joined as fifth Assistant to B. Gopal who was very busy with another film which he was finishing, and I started attending script sessions with writers Ganapathi Rao

Kommanapalli and Suryadevara Rammohan Rao on the script of *Collectorgari Abbayi*.

In the course of their script discussions with Surendra, I used to come up with ideas and suggestions which visibly impressed all three of them. Within a few days, Surendra started sending a car to pick me up, which was a huge jump up from my bus and occasional borrowed-scooter travel.

By the time Gopal was ready to shoot the film, I had risen a lot in both Surendra's and Venkat's eyes, but I had not met Nagarjuna yet. Mr Gopal and his assistants used to feel visibly uncomfortable with my proximity to the producers considering that I was merely a fifth assistant, and in those days assistant directors were expected to be very subservient.

My attitude and my speaking in English also understandably put them off; to the extent that when one day Surendra was discussing budget cuts with Mr Gopal, he suggested removing me as one of the cuts. Moreover, in just about a week, I had proved to be the worst assistant director ever, often losing clapboards and continuity books. So Surendra asked me to lay off and just hang around the set without taking on any responsibilities, which worked out fantastically for me. By virtue of being free on the set, I slowly started developing a rapport with Nagarjuna who had started shooting by then. Nagarjuna was pretty impressed with my narration skills and cinematic sense, but he himself was not in a very strong position because after the success of his first film *Vikram*, which many attributed to it being ANR's son's first film, he had a string of flops. So in the film industry, I managed to attain the status of Nagarjuna's chamcha and the worst assistant director ever, and also a guy with a huge attitude problem and no future prospects.

Meanwhile, I left my video shop to my staff and they cheated me royally and the business went for a toss. All the 'I told you so' guys reappeared and lectured me on how in chasing a foolish dream, I had gone horribly wrong.

As I was hanging out on the sets of *Collectorgari Abbayi,* Surendra came up with the idea of making a film based upon *The Sound of Music* (made as *Raogari Illu*). Since I had come in towards the end in *Collectorgari Abbayi*, after most of the script had been finalized and decisions about casting and selection of technicians already made, I thought this would be a great opportunity to be involved in a film right from the inception. By that time, while I had become close to Venkat and Surendra and Nagarjuna, they were by no means in the mood to offer me a film to direct, their basic contention being that I didn't have practical experience.

But by the force of my personality, I slowly started influencing Surendra who wanted an established director for *Raogari Illu* to take on a new director with lots of experience instead. I suggested Tarani, second assistant in *Collectorgari Abbayi,* who had around fourteen years' experience and whom

I knew well. My agenda was that if he was directing, I could be part of all the decisions right from the beginning or, simply put, I could be a backseat director. So I manipulated Surendra to decide on Tarani, which he finally did. I was ecstatic because this gave me a chance to get a ringside view of how an idea grows and shapes into a film. Little did I know how horribly wrong this would go. Tarani was initially very grateful to me as he knew that I was mainly responsible for Surendra taking him on as director, but slowly he grew tremendously irritated with what he perceived as interference on my part and which I had thought of as my creative inputs. He was also very jealous of my proximity to the actors and the producer. ANR was the star of the film and he kept a distance from everybody including Tarani. All the other actors like Jayasudha and Revathy interacted more with me than Tarani, which understandably upset Tarani. Things came to the point where Tarani issued Surendra an ultimatum that he wouldn't shoot if I was on the set. Seeing Surendra's dilemma, I offered to stay out. But the problem was that it was I who had narrated the story to the actors and Tarani was shooting it differently without being able to tell them the reasons for the changes. This created a lot of discomfort on the set.

Meanwhile, *Collectorgari Abbayi* was released and became a big hit and Nagarjuna was hot property. By that time he was keen to take a chance with me as a director, but ANR was dead against it. He told Nagarjuna, 'Just because Ramu can speak in English and quote from English novels and films, does not mean that he can direct.' Nagarjuna expressed his helplessness to me.

As this was going on, one day Tarani was shooting a key scene, and ANR had a doubt about the way the scene was structured that Tarani could not resolve. As an escape route, Tarani told him that the scene was conceived by me and approved by Surendra and that he was just forced to shoot it. ANR called for me and Surendra.

He took off on the stupidity of the scene when I stopped him and explained to him the whole point of the scene and how it should be shot. That's when ANR realized how wrongly Tarani had been shooting it, and worse that he didn't even understand the point of the scene. He asked me to be present for the shooting of the scene, and by the end of it he told Nagarjuna at home that he was mighty impressed with me.

With that, practically all decks were cleared for me to be given a break, as ANR had given the green signal. Nagarjuna was positive anyway, and Venkat and Surendra were reasonably positive although dilly-dallying. The question was when. Venkat said they were shooting a film called *Vijay* with B. Gopal, and Surendra was planning another film with Kodandi Rami Reddy starring the father and son duo again, and after that there was another project with K. Raghavendra Rao. They could think of giving me a film only after those films were over. My heart sank as I was in no mood to wait that long.

By that time I had understood enough of how the industry operated. Surendra asked me to write a story for Kodandi Rami Reddy's film which I did. He signed Ganesh Patro as dialogue writer. Kodandi Rami Reddy in those days did seven–eight films a year, and most of the time would not even remember the story of the film he was currently shooting. I digested this information and resolved to use it to further my end. I narrated the story to Mr Reddy and Mr Patro, who were fine with it. Then Surendra asked Mr Patro to go to Hyderabad from Chennai where we were at the time, to narrate it to ANR who was shooting in Hyderabad. Later that night I talked to Mr Patro and offered to go in his place. Mr Patro was only too happy to be saved the trouble, and Surendra sent me instead.

Once there, by deliberate design I narrated the story in such a way that ANR had lots of problems with the script. He called up Surendra, Mr Patro and Mr Reddy, and told them the story did not work at all. They were taken by surprise, and waited for me to come back to tell them what the problem was.

I went back and told them a completely different version of the problems ANR had, designed to confuse Mr Patro and Mr Reddy. I relied on the fact that Mr Reddy did not have a script sense and he also had a weak memory, and Mr Patro at any given point of time was busy with ten films and was primarily a dialogue writer. So I confused them to the point that suddenly they felt that they had no script for the film, and Nagarjuna's dates were just around the corner.

Leaving all three in a state of confusion, I went to Nagarjuna, who then used to live above the office, and told him that there was no script for the Kodandi Rami Reddy film and no way a script could come up in the given time. Since my script was ready and he *had* decided to take a chance on me someday, why not take it now? He asked me about what Surendra might say. I went to Surendra and told him that since he would lose a project with Nagarjuna and not get dates with him again for quite some time, I would try and convince Nagarjuna to fit my film into those dates instead. When he agreed, I met Nagarjuna and told him Surendra was keen to do the film with me and I called Surendra and told him Nagarjuna was fine with doing my film. The long and short of this convoluted story is that I made both Nagarjuna and Surendra feel that doing my film was the other's decision. But both of them said that they had to get Venkat's approval. He wasn't home but I waited until midnight and when he came in, I told him that both Nagarjuna and Surendra had decided to do the film with me. He was non-committal. In the morning, before Venkat woke up, I told Nagarjuna and Surendra that Venkat was very happy with the decision. And after Venkat woke up, I took care that no two of them met each other without my being present. There were also some undercurrents among them, which I took advantage of by making each feel that if he opposed the decision, the other two would support me.

Then I leaked out the news to the staff at the office. When Surendra was asked by a staff member if Mr Reddy's project had been shelved, I told Surendra that it could have been leaked by Nagarjuna or Venkat. I told him that he should hurry up and break the news to Mr Reddy himself before Mr Reddy got to know of it from someone else, which was bound to create bad feeling. So Surendra met Mr Reddy and told him.

The news of Annapurna Studios dropping Kodandi Rami Reddy for Ram Gopal Varma spread like wildfire, since it was the first time a big production house had opted for a rank newcomer in place of the reigning director. Finally, after ANR was formally informed, I was given the go-ahead and *Shiva*'s pre-production work started in full earnest.

I conned and lied to everybody concerned, but the one and only truth was that I genuinely believed that *Shiva* would be a far superior film to whatever Mr Reddy might make.

PS: After the success of *Raogari Illu*, Tarani made a few flops and is now back to working as an assistant director.

Chapter 9

The Biggest Thrill of My Life

WHEN I WAS IN college, I used to hang out near Vijaylaxmi theatre in Kamayyathopu, in Vijayawada district. My friends Sridhar and Naresh, and I were the three most useless bums in our college. Every day, without exception, we used to watch movies and often the same movie repeatedly. We watched repeatedly not because the film had an inspirational or fascinating story, or to study some fine cinematic detail, but for something completely base and trite like catching a glimpse of the heroine's leg or navel again, or maybe for a comic scene or an adrenalin-pumping action scene.

Coming back to Kamayyathopu's Vijayalaxmi theatre, the three of us used to stay in a room right next to the theatre, and most of the time we were broke and hence could not afford the tickets. So like vagabonds we used to hang out in the compound of Vijayalaxmi theatre, having tea and biscuits in the canteen and running up an account with the canteen guy who used to, both out of pity and irritation, give us sizeable credit, sometimes going up to ₹40.

The manager of Vijayalaxmi, who used to walk around the theatre, knew us by face as we were constantly there even during college hours. His disgust at our complete lack of purpose was often clearly reflected on his face. One day, he told me point-blank that I should be ashamed of myself for behaving so irresponsibly, and advised me to think of my parents who were working hard and had expectations of me regarding a career, while I was neglecting my studies and wasting my time on movies instead.

For approximately two days, I was suitably chastened and then I was back at my vigil at the theatre. The manager was so irritated that he would look away whenever he saw me in the theatre compound after that and in time, he began to look through me as if I was not worth his time.

For around four years, Vijayalaxmi theatre was a like a second home to me. Sometimes I used to be inside watching a movie, sometimes inside the compound looking at the posters, and sometimes at night when I had no money to buy a ticket, I used to stand at the back of the theatre to catch the soundtrack.

Years after I left Kamayyathopu and made my directorial

debut with *Shiva*, I was invited by the distributor of Vijayawada to come and see for myself the crowd reactions, after it became a blockbuster. When I arrived there and asked him which theatres the film was playing in, one of the theatres he mentioned was Vijayalaxmi.

I told him that I wanted to see *Shiva* there. Throughout the journey in an air-conditioned car from the hotel in Vijayawada town to Vijayalaxmi theatre, which was 7 km away, my mind was flooded with memories of how I used to travel in jam-packed buses on that road, and many a time walk because I had no money even to buy a bus ticket.

Meanwhile, the distributor called up Vijayalaxmi theatre to say that Ram Gopal Varma was on his way, and word got around causing a big crowd at the theatre. The owner of the theatre was there to greet me personally, holding a garland in his hands, and as I got down he put it around my neck and people started clapping. Somewhere behind the proprietor and his friends, I caught the manager's face looking at me in complete shock and disbelief. He had only known me by face and never in his wildest dreams would he have imagined that this hugely successful film had been directed by the same useless bum who used to hang around aimlessly in his theatre.

I smiled guiltily at him and as I was being taken inside, the owner asked the manager to get snacks for me from the canteen.

I turned back to look at the canteen, and the man who ran the canteen waved frantically at me over the heads of the crowd with tears of happiness in his eyes. I guiltily remembered the ₹40 I owed him of old. I told one of my guys to return his money and also give anything extra if he asked. My guy later told me that he had refused, and he just wanted a picture with me. So I posed behind the counter in the canteen with him.

As I left the theatre after watching the film, I looked around and spotted the manager in the crowd and walked up to him. He looked at me as if he was seeing a ghost. As I stretched out my hand to shake his hand, he hugged me spontaneously. That hug in the compound of Vijayalaxmi theatre was just about the biggest thrill of my life.

PS: I set the opening sequence of *Raat*, when Revathy gets off a bus, in Kamayyathopu—as a tribute to the place and also because that's where I conceived the film.

MY GODS

Chapter 10

My Sridevi

WHEN I WAS STUDYING engineering in Vijayawada, I would so often, while standing in the line to buy a ticket for the new Sridevi movie, keep staring longingly at her on the hoardings in the theatre compound.

Her beauty and sex appeal were so overpowering that it took many many films and many many years for both the audience and the industry to recognize the actress in her, who was first showcased, according to me, in the most effective way by Shekhar Kapur in *Mr India*. Even though her acting prowess was evident right from her debut film, her superstardom kind of gave prominence only to her sex-symbol image, which was so strong that it blinded everybody to her tremendous talent.

Mr India made the audience discover a new Sridevi,

primarily because of the way Shekhar Kapur aesthetically captured both her extraordinary beauty and her incredible performance.

My journey to Sridevi started when I was preparing for my debut film *Shiva.* I used to walk from Nagarjuna's office in Chennai to a neighbouring street where Sridevi used to live, and I would just stand and stare at her house. I just couldn't believe that the goddess of beauty lived in that stupid-looking house. I say stupid because I believed that no brick-and-mortar house deserved to hold that ethereal beauty called SRIDEVI. I used to desperately hope to catch a glimpse of her as she went in or out of her house, but sadly no such thing ever happened.

And then, after *Shiva* became a big hit, producer Gopala Reddy S. came to me and asked if I was interested in doing a film with Sridevi. I said 'Are you mad or what? I will die just to see her, let alone make a film with her!' Gopala Reddy arranged a meeting with her, and took me to meet her in that very same house I used to stand and stare at. We went at around 7.30 at night, and as luck would have it, there was a power cut in her house. So I was sitting in her living room in candlelight along with Gopala Reddy , waiting for the angel to appear and my heart was thumping like mad. Her mother told us she was busy packing as she was about to catch a flight to Mumbai.

As we were waiting, every once in a while Sridevi rapidly

crossed the living room as she moved from one room to another in a rush to finish her packing, apologetically smiling at me for the delay. Every time she appeared and disappeared in a flash, the director in me started slow motioning her and running her backward and forward for my visual pleasure.

Finally, she came and sat in the living room, just uttered a mandatory few lines that she would very much like to work with me, which I am sure she said to a host of other directors as well, and then she left for Mumbai. I continued talking to her mother with enormous respect and awe because she had actually given birth to Sridevi.

I went back to my place feeling like I was in the seventh heaven. The way Sridevi had sat in front of me in the candlelight got imprinted in my mind like an exquisite painting, and with her image completely filling both my mind and heart, I started writing *Kshana Kshanam*.

I wrote *Kshana Kshanam* with the one and only purpose of impressing Sridevi. *Kshana Kshanam* was my love letter to her.

Throughout the making of *Kshana Kshanam,* I just couldn't take my eyes off her. Her charm, her beauty, her personality and her demeanour were a new discovery for me. She had an invisible wall around her, and she did not let anyone cross that. Behind that wall, she maintained her dignity and her self-respect and she never let anyone inside. Also, in the course of working with her and observing her acting technique, I began to understand more and more as a director the nuances of her performances and characterizations. For me she was the epitome of cinematic acting, which I believe is many times more complex and effective than theatre acting.

When I was shooting the song 'Andanantha Ettha Tara Theeram' in *Kshana Kshanam*, after a certain shot in which Venkatesh and Sridevi were dancing, I said 'fantastic' and the dance master asked for one more take. After the shot was done, once again I said 'fantastic' and the dance master again asked for one more... I asked my assistant why he was asking for one more take, and he said, 'Sir, you are looking at Sridevi and he is looking at Venkatesh.' Well, if she was in the frame, no matter who else was there and what else was happening, I and millions of others had eyes only for her.

Her popularity and stardom had to be seen to be believed. We were shooting for the climax of *Kshana Kshanam* in Nandyal, and the whole town came to a standstill. Banks, government offices, schools, colleges, everything in town stopped functioning as everyone wanted to see Sridevi.

She was staying in a traveller's bungalow, a little distance from the bungalow where Venkatesh and I were staying. There used to be a crowd of at least 10,000, just staring at her bungalow throughout the night. There were about fifty local toughs along with a 100-strong police force continuously deployed to guard her.

When we were on location, we used to know when Sridevi had started from her bungalow to come to location, because we could see a column of dust travelling towards us from the distance. The dust was kicked up by the thousands of people running behind her car.

Well anyway, to cut the long, touching story of my feelings for Sridevi short, I finished *Kshana Kshanam* and then went on to make *Govindha Govindha* with her. In due course I saw her undergoing a lot of personal tragedy like her father's death and her mother's mental illness.

The woman who was the object of lust of the entire nation's male population, was suddenly left all alone in the world till Boney Kapoor stepped in to fill the vaccum. So, straight from her superstardom, magazine covers and her dazzling beauty on the silver screen, I saw her in Boney's house serving tea like an ordinary housewife. I hated Boney Kapoor for bringing that angel down from heaven to such an ordinary, humdrum existence.

I don't go to Boney's house these days because I can't bear to see Sridevi in a real everyday setting. For me, she is a highly precious jewel to be showcased only in exotic locales and brilliant cinematic settings.

Sridevi is one of the sexiest and most beautiful women God ever created, and I think he creates such exquisite pieces of art only once in a million years.

So what if Boney has the real Sri in his house...? I have her captured as a cinematic goddess in my mind's camera and as a divine angel in the heart of my celluloid dreams.

I thank god for creating Sridevi, and I thank Louis Lumiere for creating the movie camera to capture her beauty forever.

Chapter 11

Rahman Times

I WAS MAKING A Telugu film called *Kshana Kshanam* with a first-time music director called Keeravani, now known as M.M. Kreem. One day at the recording studio, while we were having lunch, Rickey, a rhythm programmer working with M.M. Kreem at that time, mentioned a very talented keyboard player called Dilip. That was the first time I heard of A.R. Rahman. I didn't take Rickey seriously. Much later when I happened to hear *Roja*'s songs at Mani Ratnam's house, long before the film was released, I was blown away by the sheer originality of the orchestration and tunes. I immediately wanted to sign Rahman on for a film I was making with Sanjay Dutt called *Nayak*, and another film called *Rangeela*. But my investors preferred Anu Malik, as they felt the success of the music of *Roja*'s dubbed version was a fluke, and that kind of music would not work in Hindi. The very fact that AR had not been signed up by any top Hindi filmmaker after *Roja* was proof enough, they reasoned. They felt that Anu Malik was at the top of his form after *Baazigar*, and that we would get a much bigger price for the audio with his music.

I bargained with them that I would sign Anu Malik for *Nayak,* if they allowed me AR for *Rangeela*. They agreed, but the plain truth was that they were not really interested in *Rangeela,* as Sanjay Dutt post *Khal Nayak* was a much bigger star than Aamir at that time. After twenty days of shooting for *Nayak,* Sanjay got arrested in the 1993 serial blasts case and the film was shelved. (Much later I made the same script as *Sarkar.*)

Before AR, I had worked with Ilayaraja, M.M. Kreem and Raaj Koti, and knew many other music directors on a personal level and was familiar their working styles. What struck me first when I met AR was the incredible dignity with which he carried himself. There was none of the arrogance or pride which success invariably brings out in people. After telling him the story of *Rangeela*, I gave him references of some Hollywood musicals, and described to him the visual style I was planning to capture the film in. Once he went through the situations, the compositions he came up with would surprise me, though not always pleasantly, to begin with. That is because his interpretation of the emotion of a situation was so originally captured in his tunes that they would take time to sink in for a conventional ear. That I think is the reason one tends to like his music more and more as one listens to it again and again. A case in point is the 'Hai Rama' song, where my brief to him was that I wanted to shoot an erotic number, capturing the lust in Urmila's and Jackie's faces rather than the romance.

I said to him that when animals have sex they are not ashamed or shy, as they are so completely lost in their feelings for each other, they do not care where they are or who is watching them. The visual of Urmila and Jackie circling each other in the Kuldhara ruins of Rajasthan in broad daylight was the key image I gave him.

After the brief, I was subconsciously expecting him to come up with a tune on the lines of 'I Love You' ('Kaate Nahin Katte Ye Din Ye Raat') in *Mr India*. What he came up with was the 'Hai Rama' tune, which sounded to me like some classical Carnatic raga, and my first reaction was that he had lost his mind. However, it grew on me, and I finally said that we would go ahead with the tune even though I was still unsure, deep inside, of how it would fit into the situation. But when he finished the entire track with the orchestration, it sounded sensuous beyond my wildest imagination. He captured the erotic intensity and the purity of its feeling in the beginning alaap, the cello themes and the wild tablas, magnifying the effect of the images I created many times over.

One other difference I have noticed between AR and other music directors is that whereas others pretty much dictate to the musicians and singers what they want, AR interacts with them in a way that makes each and every one of them feel as if it is their song and not his; thereby placing the onus on them to feel from within and get the best out of themselves.

Whereas most music directors record the final track first with all the orchestration, and get the singer to dub last, AR invariably gets the singer to dub on a base rhythm track first and does the orchestration later, as he wants the orchestration to rise from the depth of feeling in the singer's voice. That's the reason you can't separate the voice from the music in each of his tracks. Each and every instrument is made to play with the same emotional depth as the singer's voice.

Not knowing the technicalities of music, I would think the phenomenon of AR owes not only to his obvious talent but also to his incredible patience, focus and dedication towards his creations. Most music directors forget about a song the moment they finish recording it and move on to whatever else they are doing. AR keeps revisiting his songs and effecting changes in them (read sculpting and polishing). Until the time the tracks have to leave for the audio company, he treats each and every song of his like his own daughter whom he is preparing for marriage with the listener.

Also, AR is the only artiste I have met, who does not have creative arrogance. I mean that he never defends his work if it is being criticized. He was recording the *Rangeela* theme in Chennai while I was shooting in Mumbai. When he sent the track to me, I didn't like it on first hearing. Not just I, but the entire unit. I called AR and told him that it was not working. Without a second's pause, he said he would work out something else, and this he said after having worked on the track for more than a week.

As I was playing the theme in my car over and over again, at some point it hit me like a thunderbolt, and I told him that I must have been out of my mind not to have liked it in the first place. He smiled and said, 'I knew you would like it eventually.'

The aesthetics of his song tracks are beyond comparison with any other music director's. What I mean by aesthetics is, if the melody is the story, the various instruments and the way they are recorded, played and their inter-volume levels and tones are like art direction and cinematography. So, while purely in terms of melody, one might have one's individual favourites, his aesthetics are always perfect irrespective of the overall effect of the song.

I can never forget AR saying to me in his studio, 'I've decided that whatever goes from here has to be good.' He said it neither with arrogance nor overconfidence. It was just so very simply said, just a decision he had taken, and that single sentence made me understand his greatness more than his music itself. I have known many, myself included, who have said, thought and wished the same, but I have yet to meet another man who has put it into practice so uncompromisingly. *Jai Ho!*

Chapter 12

My Affair with Amitabh Bachchan

IN A NOT SO totally darkened theatre (because of light leaking in through some vents and gaps in the closed doors) called Ramapriya, in Vijayawada town in Andhra Pradesh, I as a film viewer, for the first time, consciously began to understand the phenomenon of Amitabh Bachchan.

The film that was playing was *Khud-Daar* and the scene at that precise moment was when Amitji comes to know of the lie his own brother has told him and barges into a discotheque where his brother is grooving away with a girl. As he shouts at the DJ to stop the music and looks at his brother in the far corner with hurt filling his eyes, a gang of vicious-looking bouncers moves towards him. He looks at them and in a voice choked with emotion says that he will break their legs if they try to stop him. There was an audible gasp in the theatre from the viewers as he said this. The interesting point is that nobody in that theatre could speak Hindi as Vijayawada is a Telugu-speaking town. So what did they connect to? It was just the mix of his raw emotions of anger, betrayal, helplessness and above all hurt that he managed to communicate through his body language, his voice and, of course, his eyes.

As I looked at the faces of the people sitting in the theatre I could see a tremendous sense of awe, admiration, respect, and above all a sense of connection. Each and every one of his viewers connected with him deeply through the characters he portrayed in his various films. Each and every one wanted a brother, a friend or a leader like him.

Even after the volumes spoken about him and big fat books written on him, I think it is still very easy to underestimate his incredible influence and his unimaginable impact not only on cinema but also on the consciousness of at least a couple of generations of Indians.

The older generation as kids loved him in *Amar Akbar Anthony*, and kids now love him in *Bhoothnath*.

As a teenager I have seen street goondas in the back lanes of Hyderabad imitating his performances in *Kaala Patthar, Deewaar*, etc., and I know of even present-day gangsters who are awestruck by his intensity in *Sarkar*.

Women used to swoon over his romantic performances then, and even today women want a life-partner like him.

Old people back then wanted a son like him, and old people today see a reflection of their own life in his performances in movies like *Baghban*. His contemporaries back then were dying of jealousy and unable to understand what made him tick and the resumés of today's stars and technicians are not complete until and unless they feature him in at least one of their films.

The difference between Amitabh Bachchan and modern-day stars is that he never needed anything other than his incredibly emotive face to connect with the audience, unlike the superstars of today who have the tremendous support of highly evolved production techniques.

If you ask any random man on the street, anywhere in the country, what he remembers of Amitabh Bachchan, he is bound to come up with at least a hundred of his favourite scenes, dialogues or moments from Amitji's various films. Whereas if asked about any of the modern-day superstars, I doubt that anyone will remember anything beyond their hit songs, and that too for a maximum of a couple of weeks, and perhaps their weekend box-office collections.

From the time of being awestruck with him in *Zanjeer, Deewaar,* etc., to consciously understanding his screen prowess post *Khud-Daar*, my biggest desire cinematically was to do a film with him, which I eventually realized in *Sarkar*. In the run-up to the making of *Sarkar,* in my several meetings with him, I started seeing a very different side of him too. Behind the obvious power and intensity, was a sensitivity and vulnerability. Listening to his thoughts made me see his incredible versatility both as a human being and as an actor. By that time my proximity to him had blunted my sensibilities as a viewer of his star performances, and the filmmaker in me got greedy and dumb enough to experiment with him as an actor, resulting in *Nishabd* and *Aag*. It's not so much the quality of those films that I am talking about here, but the idea of casting him in those roles.

Amitji's make-up man told me on day one of the shooting of *Nishabd* that the film wouldn't work, because no one was going to accept Amitji in a role like that. Whether that was the reason or not, I myself as a viewer probably wouldn't want to see him in a role like that. I think *Nishabd* is Amitji's finest performance as an actor, mainly because of the sheer complexity of the role and the subtle nuances of reactions it demanded, which most of the so-called art-house actors won't even begin to understand, let alone portray. But the question is, does one want to see Amitji just as an actor? I for one don't, unless the acting is coming from a certain larger-than-life perspective.

Similarly in *Aag,* there will be a difference between a viewer's reaction and my reaction to his performance. As a director, I judge an actor by seeing what he does with what is given to him. The viewer sees the final effect of that in the context of the film and hence, he cannot have any idea of how I could have screwed it up in the screenplay or edit, or of the various other blunders I could have committed. People seeing the film react to the effect, whereas as a director I know the cause.

On the other hand, if somebody argues that Amitji had no business doing those films without knowing what he was getting into, yes, he was guilty of misplacing his trust in me, but he was not guilty of not doing his best.

I gathered from my association with him that being the ultra-professional that he is, once he agrees to do a film, he completely succumbs to the director's vision or lack of it. The end product can sometimes look a mess, but the inside secret is that he would always have given much more than was expected of him.

When he stands on the steps looking at Aftab taking Jiah away in the climax of *Nishabd*, his close-up shot calls for an extraordinary understanding of human emotions and hence, it is a far superior performance compared to him saying '*Tujhe bhi karne nahin doonga*' in *Sarkar* which he would have done hundreds of times before. But sadly the effect of that line in *Sarkar* will become cinematic history whereas the *Nishabd* close-up shot might go unnoticed.

The point I am trying to make is that he has never ever failed as an actor and he never will. It's only directors, myself included, who frequently fail to capture his art in the right context.

Karan Johar's favourite films of his are *Kabhie Kabhie* and *Silsila,* which I don't care for much compared to my favourites like *Deewaar* and *Zanjeer*. I don't like to see him in films like *The Last Lear, Black* and *Bhoothnath.* But that's what he is all about. Amitji is an artist, who can and will allow himself to be moulded and shaped in any which way one wants, and he will leave the final result in the hands of the director he is working with.

In all my association with him, I can recall any unpleasantness on only two ocassions. One was when I was shooting the confrontation scene with him and Kay Kay, who played his son in *Sarkar,* and he disagreed with me on a certain reaction I wanted him to give. Inspite of my trying to explain, he insisted that I do it his way and I had to relent. But after the shoot, late at night he called me and said, 'Ramu, I have been thinking about it and I think you are right. Let's do it again.' Once I re-shot it and showed him the edit, he was very impressed. The good thing about it was that he developed implicit trust in me after that, and the bad thing was that it was misplaced it in the context of *Aag.*

The other famous or rather infamous incident was when I

tweeted something very abusive about him on Twitter for not continuing to do certain kinds of roles. After seeing him playing old-man, Alzheimer's-patient kind of roles for many years, I flipped on suddenly seeing the vintage Bachchan again in *Bbuddah Hoga Terra Baap*. In that frame of mind, and under the influence of three-four vodkas, I tweeted, 'Amitabh bachchan is a c*****a for not doing more roles like this and directors like me are l****s, for not realizing this.' Understandably, all hell broke loose. People and media gave me so much flak without even bothering to understand what that tweet meant. They just went by the words used without seeing them in context. The only man who immediately understood it to be a compliment was Amitji himself.

All things said and done, there's just one thing I hate about Amitabh Bachchan and that is his birthday. Every birthday of his reminds me that he is getting older and older and I hate that.

I just wish that God would realize that Amitabh Bachchan is a rare art form that even he himself can create only once in a million years and so just put him on a pause button and make him live forever.

TAKE 1: ON FILMS

Chapter 13

Stars and Actors

THE FIRST QUESTION PEOPLE ask when told to see a particular film is, 'Who is in it?' This is what star value is all about. Because they cannot know how the film is, the presence of a particular star can help people make up their minds.

The primary difference between a star and an actor is that the star is a personality. One prime example of this is Shah Rukh Khan. Whether he is in a commercial, doing a show, acting in a film or just being himself, he has the same charisma. From personal interactions that I have had with him, I have found him much more effective, entertaining and charming in person than in his umpteen blockbusters. On the other hand, an actor is playing a character and it is the character which people connect to.

At an awards function post *Satya,* when Manoj Bajpayee came on stage, people were screaming 'Bhikku Bhai' despite Shah Rukh's presence, which obviously thrilled Manoj. I cautioned him after the event not to get carried away, and to realize people were calling him by his character's name and not his own. Shah Rukh by that time might have given twenty-five super hits, but nobody remembered his character's name in any of those films. That is the power of a star. Actors die along with their characters and stars live on.

Lots of people complain that Shah Rukh does the same kind of acting all the time, meaning that he is repetitive. I believe it's precisely because of this he is such a big star. In fact, the moment anyone tries to make him do something other than be himself, they will fail. Two examples being *Paheli* and *Swades*. I think it works like this on a psychological level. If you meet a person and you like him, why the hell would you want him to change every time you meet him? At best, you will want him in different situations and in different backgrounds or interacting with different people. But he himself should never change. The prime examples of this are Shah Rukh and Rajinikanth. On the other hand, when you are making a film which revolves around extremely believable characters, a star can become an impediment because he carries along with him a baggage of image and expectations and this eats into the believability of the film. For example, if John Abraham's stardom is due to his deadly looks in *Dhoom,* why spoil it by making a film like *No Smoking* with him? The director might have got a performance out of him and he might also have done very well, but the question is whether people want to see him act or just look good. So the very star who is supposed to draw in the crowds can become excess baggage for the film.

Conversely, when you go to a DVD store and look around at the choice of films, many a time you will catch yourself picking up a film not so much for the stars, but because you like the title, the poster design or the blurb on the back of the cover. So if who is in the film can be a drawing force, what it is about can also be a drawing force.

Chapter 14

The Power of an Idea

NOTHING IS TRUER THAN the line from the Idea campaign which says, 'An idea can change your life.' My whole life, and my career as a director, is living testimony to that truth, both in positive and negative ways. *Satya* emerged from an idea, 'We always hear about gangsters only when they either kill or when they die. But what do they do in between?' At the other end of the spectrum, *Ram Gopal Varma Ki Aag* too emerged from an idea, 'What if *Sholay* is set in today's times?' We all know how differently the two ideas panned out—one resulted in a cult film and the other in a box-office disaster. But at the time they came to me, I was equally excited by both, if anything more so with the *Sholay* idea. But, irrespective of their strengths and final outcomes, the one thing they have in common is that both managed to change the trajectory of my life, though in different directions.

The story of Paritala Ravindra and Maddelacheruvu Suri had been playing out in the real world for more than a decade, and in spite of that nobody ever thought of making a film on them until I stumbled upon the idea. That *Rakhta Charitra* was a moderate success is beside the point. The fact that about 200 people worked on it non-stop for more than six months, and more than ₹30 crore was spent on it, is the point. Apart from that, at the heart of the mind space of so many people being occupied, whether of the people involved with the original incidents or of the people who just wanted to debate or discuss its proceedings or of the three marketing teams that broke their heads figuring out how to sell the concept of a film being made in two parts, was nothing but my idea, 'What if I make a film on Ravi and Suri?'

Many of my detractors wonder how in spite of the kinds of films I make, I can still go on doing exactly what I want and exactly as I wish. The secret of that is nothing but the power of the ideas I get at various points of time, my belief in them and my ability to sell them to the people who matter for turning them into films.

Many people think I work on multiple films at the same time but that is not at all true; what is true is that I work on multiple ideas at any given time. Each of them can take its own sweet time to develop into a script and then into a film, but they are constantly brewing in my head and in various others heads where I put them, namely of writers and assistant directors. For instance, I had the idea of making *Sarkar* in my head for five years before I got around to making it and I had the idea of *Ek Hasina Thi* for eight years. The moment I get an idea, I put a writer on to it, and then periodically discuss with him the progress depending on my priorities. But the moment I talk about my idea for a certain film, the media projects it as already in the works and hence it appears as if I am working simultaneously on many projects.

I am working on ten ideas which are still untitled and will take their own time to fructify. But the beauty of those ideas is that each one of them is like a ball of bundled up potential energy just waiting to go kinetic. They can each turn into anywhere between a ₹5-crore and 50-crore film when their time comes.

Recently an ad agency approached me to direct an ad film and I told them that I couldn't think of directing a 60/30 second ad with a creative given by someone else to suit the requirement of the consumer and the client (which is how the advertisement industry works).

I said that I would make a full-length movie instead with the product name. When they asked me what I meant, I said, 'For example, what if I make a movie called *Lux*. The story will be about a village girl who believes that bathing with a Lux soap will make her as beautiful as a film actress, and then, in the course of the story, she becomes a star and actually models for Lux in the climax.'

They were extremely excited about the idea as they had never ever heard of this kind of an extreme product placement before—a sort of film-in ad rather than the usual in-film ad. So taken were they with the idea that they agreed to a fantastic financial deal for me.

Whether I will make *Lux* or not is a secondary point, but I just felt like bragging about the 'Power of my Ideas'!

Chapter 15

Why Cinema Exaggerates

'If you see a beautiful woman with a pimple on her face you would think nothing of it but if an aritist draws a painting of that same woman without removing the pimple it will seem offensive. Of course there could be some people who would like the pimple being there and they will be ones who will have the same character as that of the particular artist and that in effect would reflect their own personal view of life.'

—Ayn Rand

UNLIKE IN LIFE, IN cinema when a director uses style, dialogue, background score and characterization to capture reality, he wants to enhance and beautify what could be very ordinary in real life. He is, in effect, trying to show what is, as what it could be and what it should be, and that would be his view of life. And from that very specific point of view of life, his personal art will arise. Whether his art is good or bad is subjective and depends on who perceives it and from what background.

The filmmaker's interpretation and presentation of an emotion creates a feeling in a viewer sitting in the theatre, sucking him into the director's point of view. Once the film is over, the director's view becomes a part of the viewer's view.

What a filmmaker is really saying through his film is, 'This is how I want to see things. This is what life means to me.' Very rarely is a filmmaker motivated by wanting to communicate his view of life to the audience. His intention is more to capture his personal view in a tangible way on the screen. But since cinema involves commerce and various people's time and effort, he has no choice but to make it communicable, unlike a painter who while painting would never think of what will make people buy his painting.

Since we always strive to reshape the world for our own specific purpose, we have to first identity our own individual value systems so as to have a specific personal view of everything in life in order to reshape both the world and ourselves. To an extent we can reshape ourselves both physically and mentally, but it's only from our desire to reshape the world that art arises.

For instance, if I have depicted gangsters in *Company* in a certain way, that's just my artistic interpretation of the underworld. It speaks of my desire to see a guy like Mallik, played by Ajay Devgn, in the underworld, but does not necessarily mean that there is a guy like Mallik in the underworld. Similarly in *Sarkar* what I am saying is, 'This is how I would like Balasaheb Thackeray to be,' thereby giving my personal view of him.

On the other hand, for a guy who has no personal view on anything in life, the concretized projection of his malevolent non-view towards anything and everything will serve not as energy to move forward but as a negative energy to try to pull back, on delusional moral premises, people who move forward. Unfortunately this status quoist, who argues that struggle is futile, that fear, guilt, pain and failure are humankind's predestined lot, forms the majority of the world's population.

In cinematic art, I believe that it is form that matters more than substance. In other words, how a story is told, the style in which it is captured on camera, is as, if not more, important than the story itself in determining the artistic merit of a film. The story, the scene and the actor are all separate, disparate givens, but it is how the director uses the cinematic medium to amalgamate them in his own unique style which creates the impression that results in a viewer's connect, or lack of it, with a film. This is not to argue that a director's creativity can stand in for lack of content in a film, but that cinema is much more than stark, linear narration of a story. As someone once said about a particular film, 'It's quite a nice story, but if the director did not want to apply any cinematic art to it, why did he make a film out of it?' I couldn't agree more. In that sense, the other people associated with a film—actors, cameraman, music director, scriptwriter, etc.—are primary artists whose performances are designed, fashioned and interpreted by the director in his own unique style to accomplish his own unique vision.

But for that he requires first-hand understanding of all the various arts that go into making cinema, and a very individualistic view of them combined with unusual power of abstract thought, aided above all by cinematic imagination.

Directors with this kind of tremendous vision are of course rare. Most of us, most of the time, ride on the talents of others and merely put the actors and technicians through randomly thought-out motions. This sometimes accidentally results in a great movie, but most times in a movie with clashing intentions of all concerned because there is no central thought to guide the film towards its emotional finale.

A film is at the end of the day an emotional experience. It can make you cry, it can make you laugh or it can give you a thrill. A good story gives the director a means of heightening that emotion, and a great director will enhance and beautify that emotion with his artistry. For example, if the script says, 'She is very beautiful', using cinematic application the director can make the audience feel, 'She is verrrrryyyy beautifullllll.'

Chapter 16

Directing Visions

I KEEP MEETING RANDOM people at public places like airports or functions who comment on the way I frame my films. They say things ranging from, 'I like your frames' to 'Your frames look so different' and 'Why do you frame like that?' It surprises me that even people who are not at all technical can observe such things. I think they just somewhere feel a difference even if they don't really understand what constitutes it. They might not even use the word 'frame', but I realize that's what they mean.

The film fraternity also offers very mixed opinions. Some say my frames are very unique, others that they are too exhibitionistic or unnecessarily bizarre and yet others even that they are ridiculous.

To turn to why I frame in a particular way, the first point is that no frame can ever work by itself. It is entirely determined by what is being framed and in what context, and that in turn depends on the emotional tone of the subject both in terms of the actor's expression and the emotional intensity of the scene. The cinematic image is a combination of the background, the context, the actor's expression, the lighting, and how we bring all these elements together is what finally creates the so-called frame.

If Urmila's swaying hips in *Rangeela* are being framed in a certain composition, a 1-inch zoom-in or zoom-out or a little pan here or there, can both spoil and enhance the effect. Urmila's swaying hips are the content, and the particular way I want to see them swaying will constitute my frame. Similarly in Amitji's introduction in *Sarkar*, the shadows moving on Amitji's face highlight and dramatize how intensely he is listening to the old man's story. At what pace the camera is zooming out from his face has to be in sync with the mood and tone and the tempo of the background score which I would be hearing in my head at the time of shoot. When the gun crosses in out-focus in the foreground, the cut to the wide frame of the house with a child on a tricycle is what completes the intriguing aspect of *Sarkar*. If the long shot had come before the close-up, it would have been just informative and would not have had the same dramatic effect.

The best compliment I have ever received for my framing is when someone criticized my frames, someone else shot back saying that at least my framing could be criticized, while with others you couldn't even talk about their frames.

I have often observed that anything unconventional often provokes extreme reactions. For instance, there are people who love my camera work and then there are those who hate it. Similarly, there are those who think my background scores are too loud and in your face, and then there are others who say they watch my films only for their background scores.

What I'm saying is that if you have a very specific personal point of view, then it follows that it will provoke strong reactions—both favourable and unfavourable.

Any man who is self-made and has strong personal convictions will project his thoughts and feelings in a certain specific manner, which obviously is unique to his own worldview.

Just as a man's physical survival depends on his own effort, his psychological survival depends on his own mental effort and any effort at the end of the day has to be directed. Whether you allow prevailing views to direct you or you let your vision stir up the conventional view is up to you. I, for one, made the latter choice very early on in my life with regard to everything including my own life.

I realized that we are born without knowledge, so it

follows that I have to discover both knowledge and truth, as they specifically concern me and in the way I perceive and understand things. Then, when I go about the task of translating them into a reality as particularly perceived by me, I invariably start giving direction to both myself and the people who believe in my set of beliefs.

With the knowledge I acquired and intelligence I gathered from various sources and people, on one hand, I studied the physical world and the phenomena pertaining to a man's physical existence. More importantly, I also studied from my own perspective and experiences, a man's thinking and all the phenomena pertaining to his consciousness and his subconscious. This, when expressed by me in my own way, is what I would call, for want of a better term, 'my art'.

Art does not teach. It just shows, and what it shows could be beautiful to some and ugly to others.

There is a passage in *The Fountainhead* when Howard Roark explains to Steven Mallory, the sculptor, why he has chosen him.

> Your figures are not what men are, but what men could be and what men should be. You have gone beyond the probable and made us see what is possible, possible only through you.

I might not be an artist like Steven Mallory and neither might anyone call my work art, but yes, I have a very clear-cut point of view and a clear-cut personal understanding of things, and that's why I used the term 'my art' to define my work. Nobody else need perceive it as art, but it constantly and continuously guides both my life and my films.

There's a dialogue in *Nishabd* when Amitabh Bachchan's character explains to Jiah Khan's character why he photographs the way he does, '*Duniya mein bahut se cheez saamanya hoti hain, lekin ek vyakti ka nazariya use alag bana deta hain. Yeh tasveer mera nazariya, mera ehsaas hain.*' (There are many things common in this world, but a person's perception makes him different from others. These photographs are how I view things, how I experience them.)

That pretty much is the answer to why I frame my films in a certain way. It's because that's the way I want to see whatever it is that I'm framing. And this is not only true for framing a cinematic subject, but for every other aspect of filmmaking and also the way I lead my own life. So whether it's music or characterization or subject matter or editing patterns or how I live or how I behave, all are informed by one basic premise: to quote a line from *Sarkar*, '*Mujhe jo sahi lagta hain main wahi karta hoon.*'

I am not omnipotent but with whatever limited power I have, I keep striving to direct the visions of various members of a film team like actors and technicians towards my own specific vision, and in that process many a time some people may think that I have gone blind. What they don't realize is that when one is constantly visualizing, irrespective of the consequences, there can never be blindness.

Let me give the example of a scene from *Sarkar Raj*. The reason I framed it so was because I wanted the audience to be in awe of the two men who were discussing an issue which could create a problem. My intention in doing this with both the angle and the framing was to subconsciously send a message to the audience that the problem that they were discussing could be immense and that they should be heard with utmost care, while at the same time, I was subconsciously building up Rao Saab's character.

Till date some people tell me that the way this particular scene was framed was unnecessarily bizarre, and then some others think it was fantastically captured. Whatever might be the individual truths of different people, informed by their own individual perspectives and sensibilities, I believe that had I used a conventional frame for this scene, there would have been absolutely no impact and it would not have served the intended purpose. And this is what I call 'my art' or my vision, but this will not be visible to people who are blind to my vision, and it will appear as blindness on my part to them for the simple reason that they can't or don't want to see my vision.

The camera as pen

The language of a camera is primarily broken up into compositions and movements which largely depend on the placement of actors.

I give a lot of importance to the placement of actors in a scene. To give you an example, there is a scene in *Company* when Mallik comes to meet Sreenivasan along with Chandu and Pandit. I made Mallik sit in front of Sreenivasan whereas Chandu and Pandit are sitting in the back. Mallik wears glares so as not to allow Sreenivasan to read his eyes, whereas Chandu, being new to such an atmosphere, leans forward to catch the conversation. Both Sreenivasan and Chandu have to raise their voices to be heard across the room whereas Mallik and Sreenivasan talk in lower tones as they are sitting close to each other. I placed Pandit in profile to Sreenivasan. This odd kind of placement serves to establish the hierarchical differences between the characters and determines their body language, and the camera compositions also become uniquely different.

Imagine if I had shot the same scene with all three characters sitting right in front of Sreenivasan at the table facing him. It would not have had anywhere near the same impact, even though the scene content would have remained the same. That's how important placing a subject is in the context of camera framing. But yes, the placing has to emerge from the emotional and dramatic context of the scene. This scene in *Company* is a pretty simple example illustrating my point, as it consists of very steady and still compositions. In the case of *Sarkar*, I used a lot of foregrounding movement which makes the frame more intense and energetic.

Compositions and camera movements can be applied to maximum effect in a thriller format for the obvious reason that you are constantly playing around with the audience's imagination and manipulating its emotions with what you show and what you don't show in the frame.

My vision is this that I want to direct visions and I don't want my visions to be directed for me.

Chapter 17

Lock-up Lessons

BACK IN SIDDHARTHA ENGINEERING College in Vijayawada, I used to be involved in a lot of gang fights, which were quite common in colleges during those days. I think college gang fights primarily emanate out of boredom and a lack of interest in studies. They provide excitement and adventure, and they are of course also about seeking power. The gang I headed wanted to beat up a very hot-headed guy called VT. Those days there was a tough superintendent of police called Vyas posted in Vijayawada, who was a terror. His reputation was that he would beat the crap out of any law-breaker first and ask questions later. So I came up with a plan that on the last day of the final exams, once VT came out of class after finishing the paper, we would beat him up and head to our respective hometowns, and the two-month holiday period would allow things to cool off. That was my plan. The hitch was that one of our gang members, Narsing, had an exam that was deferred to the next day. I was afraid that he would be picked up by the police after we beat up VT and left. And we could not postpone beating VT up to the next day as he was leaving for his hometown the same day. So I cancelled the operation.

Then I thought of a more elaborate plan. I carefully leaked out information in a very subtle and strategic way that we were going to beat up VT on the day of his final exam. The news reached VT, which was what I intended, and he gathered a team of people to protect him as he came out of the exam hall. This allowed us to see who his supporters were. The attack didn't happen, so VT assumed it was just a rumour and went on his way. Now I used the two-month holiday to study the people who had come out in support of VT. I neutralized most of them by, in some cases threatening them, in others befriending them, so that by the time VT came back, his support had been whittled down a lot. But his hot-headedness and guts were still a force to reckon with, and SP Vyas was still around. So I decided to use VT's ego and short temper as weapons. I made the gang cross a fence from the campus into the residential colony where VT stayed. This time round too, at the last minute, I leaked out the information so as to give him time to run away. VT ran out of his house as we were reaching. We quickly crossed back into the campus.

I was counting on VT's temper and the hurt to his ego at having been forced to run like a coward to do my job for me, and sure enough VT soon rode into campus on a scooter along with a guy from his gang. He was armed with a knife and straightaway lunged for me. A friend of mine, Ravinder, came in between us and got stabbed. As we had sticks and rods, we beat up VT who ran and hid inside a room along with the bloody knife. I stood guard outside with another friend. Meanwhile, VT's gang member ran away. The police came and arrested us along with VT, and put us in two separate lock-ups at Patamata police station. I lied to the cops and implicated all of VT's supporters who had refused to cross over to my side in the attack. The fact that my friend Ravinder had been stabbed and VT caught red-handed with the bloody knife, turned the case totally in our favour. The police believed my story. They slapped a case of attempt to murder on VT and arrested all the guys whose names I had given on charges of assault. So in one master stroke, I managed to finish the opposition gang. We were released from lock-up after our statements were recorded. VT's parents came and pleaded with me to get Ravinder to take back his complaint and get VT off the hook. I complied and VT was released on bail.

But the point I want to make relates to a conversation I overheard while I was in lock-up, which taught me one of the most important lessons of my life.

A sub-inspector of police was talking casually on phone to some friend of his and mentioned in passing that some kids had been quarrelling at Siddhartha College so the police had brought them in. The incredibly bored tone in which he said it suddenly brought into focus for me how small everything really is in the larger scheme of things. Beating up VT which we had felt to be of such importance, the months of planning that had gone into it, Ravinder being in hospital with a stab wound, VT charged with attempt to murder—everything seemed so trivial when seen from the point of view of the sub-inspector who probably saw much more serious cases, day in and day out. We had created a world centred on just VT and us, and for all practical purposes the fight with VT was a world war for us.

As I thought about it, I slowly started realizing that there is no fundamental difference between two kids at school fighting over a pencil, and India and Pakistan fighting over Kashmir. It's just the arms and scales that differ. What happened to VT and me at college seemed small to the sub-inspector at Patamata police station. What happened at Patamata police station would seem trivial to SP Vyas, who headed Vijayawada police; what happened at Vijayawada would seem small from the perspective of Andhra as a whole, India as a whole, and so on. As we keep cutting to the perspectives of people with different agendas and priorities, nothing is truly important any more. So, as it happened to the Buddha under the Bodhi tree, wisdom dawned upon me in the Patamata police lock-up.

The second time I was in lock-up was at Panjagutta police station in Hyderabad, when a raid was conducted on all video libraries, including mine, based on a complaint filed by A. Purnachandra Rao, the producer of Amitabh Bachchan's *Aakhree Raasta*. The raid was to find out if we had pirated versions of *Aakhree Raasta*, and 800 video cassettes were seized from my shop. In those days, pirated versions of new films usually had fictional labels on them. So, the only way for the cops to find out was to check all the cassettes physically. While they were doing so, I was in lock-up. The difference this time compared to Vijayawada was that my folks at home had come to know, and the tension and humiliation for them was unbearable. As my cousins used some influence to get me out as fast as possible, I spent just the night in lock-up. It was not so much being inside that bothered me as the tension of the folks. Sometime around midnight, a pickpocket was brought to the police station and literally thrown into the same lock-up. He just calmly stretched himself, nodded at me, took off his shirt and, using it as a pillow, went to sleep comfortably in a corner. I just sat up the whole night and, at one point of time after the inspector had gone home, I saw all the constables gather in one room. It took me a while to realize that they were watching a blue film which they had seized in the raid.

I dozed off and woke up to find to my surprise, the pickpocket and a constable sitting on the floor on either side of the bars, sipping tea and chatting about their families. If you took out the bars separating them, they could just have been two friends. Later the inspector, talking to me, said, 'These rich bastards, the producers, cheat on income tax, earn lakhs and crores and they are after poor guys like you earning a few hundreds for your livelihood.' The human being in him connected better with my need and that of the other video pirates than with the legality of the producer's case; and he went out of his way to help me and the other pirates be let off.

So no matter whether it was a video pirate like me, the pickpocket with whom I shared the lock-up, the producer Purnachandra Rao, the constables watching the blue film, the cop sharing his problems with the pickpocket or the inspector who sided with me because of his hatred of the rich, we were all human beings at the end of the day, irrespective of uniform, job, responsibility and stature. Having been in there twenty-four hours, after I got out I developed an interest in the functioning of a police station and became close to the inspector. He shared both his on-the-job experiences and his perspectives on crime at a human level with me, often allowing me to hang out at the police station just to study and observe the happenings there.

These experiences allowed me to understand the psychology of criminals and cops, which was later reflected in my films. So the two times I was in the lock-up I would say have majorly contributed to my understanding of human psychology and behaviour, and as I already had a cinematic bent of mind it was inevitable that I dramatically drive that understanding far deeper through the use of the film medium. More than the lessons in civil engineering, I would say those lessons in the lock-up were truly an education.

Chapter 18

My World

YOU SEE WITH YOUR sense of sight, hear with your sense of hearing, feel with your sense of touch. And all these senses are nothing but functions of your mind, and the mind is nothing but a thought which is an idea.

So when you close your eyes and go to sleep, the world ceases to exist and it comes back to you when you wake up in the morning, and it is experienced in different shapes and forms by every living being on the planet. It follows that each and every one of us has our own world which cannot really be seen or experienced by anybody else no matter how close they are to us.

This world of each of us is made up of a combination of our own individual experiences, sensibilities, knowledge and intelligence, however small, big or different they might be.

So my world is nothing but a collection of my own feelings and thoughts and ideas, and it will be a fallacy for me to think that anybody else can really appreciate them, at least in the way I mean them. At best I can hope for a few others to connect to some of my thoughts in their own individual ways. This is what I mean when I say I make films for myself.

So, as long as I am sure that no one can really understand what I stand for, what is the point of even attempting to make them understand? I might as well just give an open invitation to my world through my films to whoever is interested and after that leave it to them to interpret in their own ways.

My film is nothing but my world. Many others may contribute to its shape and form but that world is eventually coloured by my vision. As a director, I am not a primary artist in the true sense of the word. Primary arts are about an actor acting, composer making music, somebody writing dialogue, etc. But all these primary arts I amalgamate into a coherent whole that creates an emotional impact or whatever else I might choose to create.

So, you will get to see the characters such as I want you to see them, hear music such as I want you to hear it. Because of this understanding of mine, I have always believed that the successes of my films belong to everybody in the team but the failures belong to me and me alone. This is because each and every artist and technician has contributed to the best of their ability as required by that portion of my world that I wanted to create in that particular film, and only I know which contribution of theirs has enhanced which part of the film. But if any visitor ventures into my world and does not like it, that is completely my failure alone.

Anyway, coming back to my worldly gyan, as long as you are sure of what your own world is, understand it and how you want to shape it and live in it, life more or less becomes a fantasy and you can have one hell of a time, the way I do.

My world consists of powerful people, intense music, sexy women, vodka, gangsters, ghosts and philosophies which I can twist and turn to my convenience.

As for the other realities of life like social responsibilities, family values and various such lofty ideals, I just close my eyes and go to sleep...

Chapter 19

The Women in My Filmy Life

OVER THE YEARS, THE media has linked me with many women, partly because I have a tendency to cast some of them again and again in my films. But then I work again and again with many male actors and technicians too. But I guess since women make more interesting copy, the media always focuses only on that aspect of my interactions. Having said that, I have to admit that some of the media speculations are true and some untrue...but, out of respect for the privacy of my heroines, I am not going to specify which ones are true and which are not.

The first heroine I was bowled over by was Sridevi and that was when I was just a viewer and hadn't yet come into films. When I first met her, I felt I had walked from the theatre straight into the screen. Over a period of time, I became close to the real Sridevi and for the first time consciously understood the difference between fantasy and reality. Post coming into films, the first girl to have an impact on me was Urmila Matondkar. I was mesmerized by Urmila's beauty—from her face to her figure…everything about her was just divine. She had done a few films before *Rangeela*, which hadn't done well and *she* hadn't made much of an impact on the audience either. Then, after *Rangeela*, she became the nation's sex symbol. That doesn't mean it was I who made her look beautiful. I would say that she was a painting and I simply framed her. Apart from the frame, for a painting to be truly relished, it also needs the right place for it to be displayed in, and that place was *Rangeela*.

One of my primary motives in making *Rangeela* was to capture Urmila's beauty eternally on camera and to make it a benchmark for sex symbols. I would say that I have never felt more of a cinematic high than when I watched her through my camera on the sets of *Rangeela*.

I don't know how this may sound, but my biggest problem with Urmila on a personal front was that I just couldn't accept her being an ordinary human being. I know that is a very unrealistic expectation from any woman, but then you have to understand that I am a very filmy person. She was, in person, a simple sweetheart, but I very selfishly always wanted her to be larger than life even in real life.

I was intrigued by the intense realism I saw in Antara Mali's face while shooting *Mast* and I thought that would work very well for her role in *Company,* which it did. But the biggest blunder I made with regard to Antara, cinematically speaking, was trying to make an Urmila out of her in *Naach*. Everyone is unique, and the problem occurs when they are portrayed in ways that don't bring out their natural selves. I believe that *Naach* would have been an entirely different film had I made it in a way that showcased Antara's natural perfection.

Of all the actors I have introduced, the one I truly feel guilty about is Nisha Kothari. I still remember the first time I saw the cute, innocent, wide-eyed girl from Delhi whom I cast in the film *James*, which I produced. While *James* was being made, I was directing *Sarkar* and I cast Nisha in a small but very memorable role in it, in which she was really appreciated. My big mistake with regard to Nisha was to weigh her down with the role of Basanti in *Aag,* my remake of *Sholay*. It's another matter that in *Aag*, I let down even great actors like Amitabh Bachchan, Ajay Devgn and Sushmita Sen; but for an upcoming actor like Nisha it was really damaging. Whether out of arrogance or overconfidence or plain foolishness, I made her suffer a crippling blow to her career and I still feel tremendously guilty about it.

When I first met Jiah Khan I thought she was the most innocently sexy girl I had ever seen. Later, when Amitji and

I were discussing *Nishabd,* I told him I had the perfect girl for the heroine's role. The moment he saw her pictures, he too agreed.

Throughout the making of *Nishabd,* the entire unit, myself included, thought that she would become a big star. Even after the film failed, because of the hype generated around her, she got roles in big films like *Ghajini*; in spite of their huge success, her career strangely never took off. When I heard of her suicide, I cried uncontrollably though I was never really close to her. She was one of the few people who couldn't cope with the disappointments and frustrations the film industry is replete with.

Of course, there are many more women I have interacted with, both on a personal and professional level, in my very long career and each and every one of them has had an effect on me in one way or the other. Today, some of them like me and some hate me, with equally good reason.

Actually, my primary worldview of women in general is as fantasy images and that's why I so absolutely love women who display their beauty on screen.

While on the subject, I find it highly objectionable to use beautiful women like Katrina Kaif, Aishwarya Rai Bachchan and Deepika Padukone to draw attention to ugly diseases like AIDS and cancer. I think the only redeeming feature of this ugly world full of disease, destruction, violence and death is that God has created beautiful women. They are the only solace in this otherwise ugly world, and I think that it's our duty towards nature and God to strive to keep a woman's beauty away from ugliness so that it can be framed, protected and worshipped.

TAKE 2: ON LIFE

Chapter 20

Happy Deathday

YEARS AGO, WHEN I was still married, I had to travel from Hyderabad to Chennai for work related to a film I was making at that time. My wife asked me not to go as the next day was her birthday. When I told her I had to, she asked me if the work was more important than her birthday. I turned around and asked her what was so important about her birth in the first place. I told her, 'I don't celebrate my own birthday inspite of having achieved whatever little I have, whereas you have achieved nothing so why do you want to celebrate your birth? If you think the mere fact that you were born calls for celebration, don't forget that when your parents had sex, the last thing they would have had on their minds while doing it was to conceive you in particular. Your dad had a desire and your mom obliged, and it was sheer accident that the particular spermatozoa which managed to enter your mom's womb just happened to be you. Your dad could alternatively have gone to a prostitute and the particular spermatozoa through which that woman might have conceived could have been you and you could have ended up in a brothel. In effect, when you have absolutely no control over or no contribution to the process of what, who and why someone gave you birth, why should you make such a big deal about celebrating it?'

Needless to say, she slapped me.

I believe that the obsession with birthdays is primarily a function of the fear most individuals have that their existence might not matter to anybody else. So on that one particular day if an X number of people greet them, it makes them feel like stars for at least that day and then they can wait like nobodies for another year to go by to become stars for yet another day.

Incidentally, the best birthday greeting I have ever received was in the form of an sms from an unknown number: 'Hey Ramu, *tere zindagi ka ek aur saal khatam...Marte Raho*!'

This sms kind of sums up my own feelings about birthdays. A birthday greeting only serves as a truly ugly reminder that I am getting that much older and that much closer to death, and consequently have that much less time to do whatever I want to do.

If at all anyone needs to celebrate, they and their near

and dear ones should celebrate their achievements and not the fact of their birth. I would rather someone close to me celebrate the day I conned a producer to give me a break in a film, than the day that I just happened to be born the way millions of people, animals and insects are born every day.

So, in effect, I am hoping that all you non-achievers who read this will cringe the next time you are looking forward to celebrating your birthday or when someone greets you with a 'Happy Birthday'.

With my brother and sister

With my assistants, all big directors now

With my favourite villain, Raghuvaran

With Sanjay Dutt on the sets of Daud

Trying to become Bruce Lee

'Can you leave the fighting to me?' says Nagarjuna

I always had a gangster in me

Checking if I look as good as Venkatesh, sitting next to Sridevi

With Sridevi on the sets of Kshana Kshanam

Made up as Dawood Ibrahim

Made up as Osama

Made up as Veerappan

With Chiranjeevi

Scared to look into Sridevi's eyes

I am a bigger fan of Sridevi than this fan

Explaining a shot to Sridevi while Prabhu Deva (then a choreographer) looks on

With media baron Ramoji Rao

Receiving an award from Amma (Jayalalithaa)

Chapter 21

Work

WE ARE BORN, LOOKED after by our parents, go to school, spend years getting educated without having the faintest idea what education means. We only realize the value of the so-called education when we are supposed to apply it in a practical sense, when most of us find ourselves pretty much lost. That is because most of us are pushed by our parents to acquire marks, never an education.

To get marks we memorize, copy and do only exam-oriented study. Even the studious, hardworking types have no thought or idea of the purpose of their education. It amazes me that throughout my growing years, not once did my parents or teachers tell me that the purpose of education is to acquire knowledge and marks are just the proof to the outside world that you do have that knowledge. The thrust on marks is because they are considered a passport to good jobs. Once they've got you that job, there is pressure to work hard in much the same way as there was pressure to study hard. My grandfather who was a civil engineer would always push me to study hard and then, when I had a job in the construction of the Krishna Oberoi hotel in Hyderabad, to work hard. He would tell me proudly that he woke up at 4.00 a.m. every day of his life. When I asked him how come some guys who woke up at 10.00 a.m. were more successful than him, he would get mad at me.

I wanted to tell him that it's success that matters, not how disciplined you are. But I was afraid of him as he was a strong man and pretty liberal with his slaps. I believe that if you are constantly doing what you are doing, just because you are told to do so, or because of your fear of the morrow, or because of commitments and responsibilities, you have lost the whole purpose of being alive.

Life is but a cycle: we are born, we grow up, we get married, we have children, we bring them up, we get them married, we become old and we die. God or nature, whatever you like to call it, gave us life to just as surely take it away, and since it is so, why not just make the best of it while we have it?

People close to me keep telling me that I work too hard. The truth is I have never worked in my life. Work is something

I define as what you have to do. But if you want to do it, it becomes a pleasure and I have always done only what I wanted to do. Society programmes us through religious strictures and moral obligations into feeling guilty about doing whatever we love to do.

As long as death is inevitable, there is no question of permanent success. Life itself is a process. For example, there is remarkable similarity between my state of mind in my college days when I sometimes had problems raising ₹40 and today when I have a problem raising ₹4 crore for a film. Everybody thought I made a bad film in *Drohi*, but it's only because of *Drohi* that I met Urmila and it's only because of Urmila I made *Rangeela*. It's only because of Sanjay Dutt's arrest that a film of mine called *Nayak* got shelved, and then years later resurfaced as *Sarkar*. So, in effect, everything in life is connected. Current success can carry the seeds of impending failure and vice versa. As long as everything is so uncertain, why worry about it and why not just do what you feel like doing every single moment of your life?

'Forget yesterday, live today and fantasize tomorrow' is the motto of my life and has always been: as an unruly kid, as an irresponsible youngster and as an erratic and eccentric adult.

My grandfather wanted me to buy a piece of land in Jubilee Hills with the ₹2 lakh I got for my first film in order to secure my future, but I went ahead and spent it on the interior decoration of a rented office which I was supposed to vacate in a few months' time. My grandfather predicted that I would be a massive failure because of this attitude of mine. Throughout his life, he worked very hard without ever questioning what exactly he was working towards. I didn't try to explain to him that the few months' pleasure I would get from the redecorated office was worth the feeling of uncertainty regarding the future.

If all your life is geared towards securing yourself against failure and death, and you never stop to enjoy the present, why live at all?

Chapter 22

A Tragicomedy

YEARS AGO, I WAS involved in a train accident while travelling from Hyderabad to Naraspur for the shooting of a Telugu film called *Prema Katha.* This accident, which resulted in seventeen deaths, was one of the most dramatic, comic and tragic experiences of my life. I know the word comic seems insensitive and out of context, but let me explain.

It was midnight and I was sleeping on the upper berth in a first class cabin when I suddenly heard a huge rattling sound, and at the same time moans from a person sleeping in the lower berth, steadily rising in volume. My first thought was that the train was off track and would crash when the moaning reached its crescendo. (I have this affliction of constantly living in a state of film irrespective of the situation.) Both the rattling and the moaning stopped as suddenly as they had begun and there was complete silence. It was pitch dark and for a few seconds I thought I must have been dreaming.

Then I tried to get up and couldn't as my head was being pressed against the wall of the coach. It took me some time to figure out that this was because the coach was on its side, inclined at about 45 degrees. With great difficulty I managed to get down and started searching for my shoes. As I wore them I heard faint whispers of people asking each other whether they were alright.

Slowly, I managed to reach the coach door. There was a very faint moonlight outside. As I stepped out, my shoe sank into the slush of a paddy field. My first thought was, 'Yuck, my shoes are f****d.' I had bought this new pair of shoes just the previous day. Once I got over my annoyance at ruining my shoes, I looked around to see a couple of coaches lying on their sides and people slowly crawling out through the connecting doors of the coaches which had broken in the accident. I walked to the track which was about 20 feet from the train as it was dry there. By that time, people were coming out.

The initial reports were that nobody was killed or hurt. One guy got a bedsheet and pillow from inside the train, put it on the tracks and instructed people around to wake him up when the rescue train arrived.

The night was full of sounds, of people crying and, strangely enough, also laughing. As I walked towards coach S5, in which most of my unit was travelling, I saw a man with a severed leg on the grass. I realized that the 'no deaths, no injuries' news was false. As I went further I saw a badly mangled coach just before S5 and I heard a man inside it moaning in pain and asking for water. It was too dark to see inside through the window but I could make out that he was somehow trapped. A guy walked up to the window with a water bottle to hand it to the poor fellow through the window when somebody else shouted at him not to give it. The guy with the water bottle turned to ask him why, and was given gyan on why an injured person should never be given water. While the man inside the train moaned in pain and begged for water, the two outside debated the wisdom of giving it to him.

'Sir, are you fine?' someone shouted from the back and I turned to see E. Nivas (the guy who made *Shool* and *Love Ke Liye Kuch Bhi Karega*), who was my assistant at the time. He was supposed to be in S5. I asked him about the rest of the crew. He answered, 'Mostly fine but Vidya is out.' I knew even when he said it, what he meant, but I thought it strange to use cricketing terminology to describe a person's death. Vidya was a camera assistant, who had been recommended to me by my cousin Shekar who was very close to him. Niwas told me that it took him twenty minutes to come out of the coach. He was sleeping in the lower berth, and after the accident he tried to move Vidya on the upper berth and couldn't, and then realized he was dead.

I took out my cell phone, which was working, and called up Shekar in Mumbai. After I told him Vidya was dead, my cousin sleepily asked, 'Are you sure?' I stopped short because I realized that I was just conveying what Niwas had told me. I asked Niwas, 'Are you sure?' This made Niwas also unsure and he said, 'He was not moving, for sure.' I said, 'Maybe he is just unconscious.' This made Niwas even more unsure, and so Niwas and I trudged through the slush to coach S5, which was lying at a 60 degrees incline. We went under it and Niwas started shouting Vidya's name through the window grill and I heard a moan. I turned sharply to Niwas and said, 'He's alive,' to which Niwas replied, 'That's not Vidya, it's Murthy.' I asked who Murthy was and Niwas said he was just a friend they had made in the coach the previous night and he was sleeping in the middle berth right below Vidya. Murthy was also apparently trapped.

Niwas started shouting at Murthy to nudge Vidya to see if he was alive. Murthy's returning moans from the darkness became a character, and I was giving Niwas my directions in soft whispers, almost feeling guilty about using this new character, Murthy, as a medium for finding out Vidya's state. So it was a three-way conversation with my whispers translating into Niwas's shouts and Murthy groaning in reply, and all of us listening to Vidya's silence.

Suddenly, a cheerful voice said from behind me, 'Varmaji you are also here?' I turned to see a man with a group of people walking towards me. I couldn't recognize him. He realized that and introduced himself as a railway officer I had met during the shooting of the climax of *Kshana Kshanam*. He had come on the rescue train and started introducing his colleagues, 'We have all come here to do the needful. This is station supervisor Ramchandran, this is my close friend Venkateshwarlu....' Then he asked me 'Can we do anything for you?' I said, 'Sir there's a unit member of mine called Vidya trapped inside this coach. Can you help in finding out whether he's alright?' He assured me he would do the 'needful' when suddenly a voice from behind us said, 'Are you suspecting sabotage?' We turned to see a reporter with a dictaphone. Suddenly the officer became very authoritative and told him, 'First we have to attend to the needful. But any information you need, you should ask only me. My name is Rao.' I could see that Mr Needful wanted to see his name in the paper the next day.

Meanwhile, a farm labourer from a nearby village was excitedly carrying on about how nothing like this had ever taken place near his village before. I could imagine Mr Excited relating it to his children and grandchildren till his dying day.

I left Niwas and the Production Manager Giri to attend to the rest of the unit and along with a unit member started walking towards a jeep to take me to Guntur, a nearby town, on Mr Needful's instructions. As I was walking, many officers and passengers who recognized me, greeted me with great respect. I reached the jeep, got in and told the driver to move. He gave me a dirty look and pointed to the wheel which was stuck in the mud and then he took off on the officers for not listening to him when he had predicted that the jeep would get stuck. He was least bothered about me or the accident. I had no choice but to trudge with some unit members through the paddy field towards a nearby village, which was probably Mr Excited's village. After I had walked a certain distance, I turned back to see the train on its side and a tree on the right between the train and me. I wished it had been a little to the left so as to present a better visual(remember my affliction!)

Once we reached the village, there were some vehicles. A friend of my friend from Guntur took me in his vehicle to his house. He was completely in awe of me and was hospitality personified. I got down in front of his house in unbelievably dirty clothes and shoes, and asked for water to wash my feet. Mr Hospitality insisted I come in. So I went into the living room to be confronted by a woman who couldn't control her anger looking my dirty feet. Mr Hospitality introduced her as his wife and she screamed at him asking why he couldn't have got my feet washed outside. He shouted back, 'Do you know who he is?' I volunteered to go out again to which she replied, 'What's the point now you've already made the floor dirty.' Now Mr Hospitality wanted me to sit on the sofa and from the look in her eyes I knew that any such action on my part would spell mortal danger for both of us. I stomped both my feet down literally and said I was not doing anything except cleaning myself up.

Once I got cleaned up, I shifted to a nearby hotel where most people from the accident had been put up. Niwas called me and told that Murthy had stopped speaking. Both of us were silent and avoided the 'death' word.

The S5 coach was so mangled that they had to cut open the top. Now it so happened that Vidya was right below the roof as he was in the upper berth. In the process of cutting the roof, his face got completely burnt from the heat of the welding torch. Whether he had died before or during this process is anybody's guess.

My cousin Shekar called me en route from Mumbai and said Vidya's father was coming and I had to break the news about his son's death to him. He'd only been told that Vidya was injured. I felt terrible that I was meeting this man for the first time in my life and I had to tell him that his son was dead. I confided my discomfiture to Pandu, a relative of mine who had come to check on me after the accident. He offered to take charge and I wondered how he would.

When Vidya's father walked in fearfully, not knowing what

to expect, Pandu slapped him sharply on the back and said in a loud, cheerful tone, 'Your son is very lucky. God loves him and so took him away. We are all bastards and I don't know when we will get that lucky.' I was shocked at the way Pandu broke the news. Vidya's father was startled both by the news and the way it was told to him. My first reaction was that it was very insensitive, but on second thoughts I thought it the perfect way of breaking news like that. Pandu went on talking about God, not giving thinking and feeling time to Vidya's father. Pandu was instinctive but I think he was more of a philosopher and psychiatrist than anybody else I've ever met.

Later I sat with Vidya's father and told him not to let Vidya's mother see his burnt face. 'Let her remember him the way he was.' He said that he couldn't do that because Vidya was her only son and I got angry with him for not being persuaded by my logic.

However, my cousin called to tell me that by the time he reached his place along with the body, Vidya's father had decided to go by my advice. He got the body cremated without Vidya's mother seeing his face. The triumph I felt about my persuasive powers overwhelmed the tragedy of the accident.

Anyway the one truth the crash brought home to me was, 'Life is really a comedy dressed up as a tragedy.'

Chapter 23

Rifle

THAT WAS WHAT WE called her. Rifle was the name someone from college gave her and it stuck. She was the sexiest woman I have ever seen in my life. When I was studying in Siddhartha Engineering College, Vijayawada, there used to be lot of construction activity going on there and she was one of the construction labourers. My classmates and I used to watch her through our classroom window while a boring soil mechanics lecturer droned on. It didn't make a difference to us that her thighs were caked with cement dust and her hair was uncombed. She walked barefoot with her chest thrust out and looked straight into our eyes. She had more sex packed in her little finger than most women have in their whole bodies. To us, she was sex personified. Imagining how she looked under her clothes drove us insane with desire. Agreed that we were at an age that even a telephone pole wrapped in a saree would have looked sexy to us, there was really something truly, amazingly, electrifyingly sexy about Rifle. It's not as if there were no other women on campus. There were plenty both in the engineering and the medical colleges, but Rifle was Rifle.

I've always felt there is a fundamental difference between beauty and sexuality. Beauty pleases your senses whereas sexuality controls your senses, or more correctly, makes your senses go wild. You lose your rational thinking and your animal instinct takes over. Rifle used to draw out the animal in all of us. With her complete indifference to us and the way she carelessly draped her saree around herself, she epitomized the word 'sex' for us. We would all sit at night with textbooks on our laps and have endless discussions on the shape and size of Rifle's assets. It took the combined strength of our upbringing, education, social programming, morality, religious strictures and fear of law to just about control us from pouncing upon her.

If ever in my life I respected God, it was for creating Rifle.

Now why was she so sexual compared to the crystal-clean girls who used to come to college in stylish dresses, their lips red with lipstick? I think it's because no man wants to taste lipstick when he kisses a girl.

I strongly feel that sexuality works more when it is ultra-real rather than when it is enhanced by cosmetics. Aesthetics kind of undermines the rawness of sex. For example I think the difference between an erotic film and a porn film is the backlighting. If it's backlit it's erotic and if it's frontlit, it's porn. In both cases, the content is the same.

All said and done, for me Rifle was the prototype of what God really intended a woman to be, before the cosmetics industry, costume designers and jewellery merchants came in and started backlighting that wonderful species called woman.

PS:

1. Incidentally Rifle never knew that she was called 'Rifle'.
2. She was completely unaware of the volcanic upheavals she aroused in the hearts and loins of a thousand guys on the campus.
3. She never knew the floodgates of jealousy she opened when she married a guy who used to run a paan shop opposite our college gate.
4. Someday I will make a film based on the concept of 'woman as a sexual being' and call it *Rifle* as a tribute to her.

MY FILMS

Chapter 24

Tough Guys Are Sexy

FROM A VERY YOUNG age I've had a fascination for tough guys, rivalled only by my fascination for women's thighs. In fact, I've always believed that men are about power and women are about sex and everything else about them is just a function of religious, social and moral programming.

Coming back to the tough guys, even back in primary school, I used to look up to the bullies in class who pinched other students and pulled their hair as they were my earliest exposure to violent power. I then slowly graduated to street goondas who beat up people and then to gangsters who shoot people and then to terrorists. When I was doing my B.Tech in Siddhartha Engineering College in Vijayawada, I had a tough-guy reputation. The irony was that I never beat up anyone myself, but I managed to create the impression among my fellow students that I could, if need be. In other words, I managed to con people into thinking I was a tough guy. Around six really tough guys who were part of my gang knew that I wouldn't be able to stand even one single punch in a real fight. But in spite of that I was their leader, and the reason for this was that I made each one of them believe that the other five would violently defend me if a problem arose. So for the outsiders, because of those six guys, I was a formidable force and for each one of the six, because of the other five together, I was a formidable force. All I had to do was to take care that they had no reason to get together behind my back. Anyway, this is pretty much the basic principle on which all street gangs, underworld factions and even political regimes operate.

Most of my understanding of the politics of violence and criminal psychology which I extensively used in films like *Shiva, Satya, Company,* and *Sarkar* came from my experiences in my college days and not from my underworld contacts as popularly believed.

The plot line of *Shiva* was a direct rip off of Bruce Lee's *Return of the Dragon*, in which Lee comes from Hong Kong to work in a Chinese restaurant in Rome where the local goons are trying to intimidate the owners. As he tries to take care of them and fight the goons, they get tougher and tougher and in the end he has a one-on-one fight with Chuck Norris in the Colosseum. In *Shiva*, Nagarjuna comes from another town to a college where the local goons are intimidating the students. As he tries to take care of them and fight the goons, they get tougher and tougher and in the end he has a one-on-one fight with Raghuvaran on top of a building. So much for originality!

The shooting went off quite uneventfully and the trouble started only after the final edit. When we arranged a projection, two outsiders who were not involved in the making saw the film and said it was too slow and boring with no drama. That was a bit of a dampener in spite of my assuring all concerned that it was the lack of background score and sound effects which was making it look like a silent film. In those days such underplayed performances and subtlety were unusual and everybody was, understandably, a bit sceptical. Nagarjuna was the only person who understood and stood by me like a rock throughout.

When the film's first trial took place, many distributors felt it was too violent and feared that women and family audiences would stay away. That would have made for disaster as they are believed to constitute the majority of the film audience.

The film was released and the first-day report the producer got from a distributor was that the audience was watching the movie silently without any reaction. We couldn't make out what that meant, till the same guy called again in the night and told us that he had finally figured out the reason for the silence; the audience was simply stunned.

Shiva created a furore at the box-office, and I became a household name in Andhra Pradesh.

Later on, it was remade in Hindi.

Some Shiva trivia

1. Originally, *Shiva* was the name of the villain in the script. In the story development stages, Nagarjuna liked the name so much, he asked me to name his character Shiva.
2. I named the villain Bhavani because I based his character on a guy called Radha with a very violent reputation in Vijayawada. Since Radha is a girl's name, I named the villain Bhavani which is a girl's name too.
3. Throughout the shooting, I wasn't too sure how the cycle chain-breaking scene would be received because after I got the idea I tried breaking a cycle chain and realized the impossibility of it. But I told myself that since nobody would have tried it, it just might look believable. After all these years the number of people who still come to me and claim that they broke a cycle chain after watching *Shiva* shows how one's imagination can take over and make one believe that imaginary is real.
4. I read about the steadicam in *American Cinematographer*

and while talking of it admiringly to a camera assistant in the studio was shocked to learn of the existence of a steadicam in Chennai for four years that nobody was using. I wanted to use it but my cameraman was reluctant saying that one couldn't centre it or balance it. I told him if we were using it in a chase scene as a point of view it wouldn't matter. Thus, I became the first director ever to use a steadicam. Within a year of *Shiva*'s release, more than ten steadicams were imported.

5. Most fight sequences in *Shiva* were choreographed by me and that is why you see Nagarjuna hitting mostly with a hook or stomach punch. That's because I knew only those two punches from my boxing days.
6. The first-ever compliment I ever got in my life as a director from an outsider was when Ilayaraja was doing the background score for *Shiva* in Mumbai, owing to a strike in Chennai at that time, a violin player walked up to me and said, 'The film is fantastic.' His name was Ismail Durbar and he later went on to give music for *Hum Dil De Chuke Sanam*, *Devdas*, etc.

Chapter 25

My Marriage to the Underworld

Satya

When I first came to Bombay from Hyderabad to shoot *Rangeela*, I couldn't get over the experience of a train ride through Dharavi. To me it looked like one single roof and I couldn't believe that people actually lived there. I saw two-year-olds crawling just about 3 feet away from the railway track where trains were rushing to and fro. I was fascinated by the busy, business-like atmosphere of Bombay (now known as Mumbai) as a whole and just couldn't wait to make love to it with my camera.

The word 'underworld' came up from time to time in conversations. I obviously also read about Dawood Ibrahim and his association with the 1993 serial blasts in the papers. But I never consciously thought about what exactly the underworld was.

Then one day, I was sitting in producer Jhamu Sughand's (the producer of films like *Rangeela, Hum Dil De Chuke Sanam*) office and he got a call that music baron Gulshan Kumar had been shot dead.

A shocked Jhamu told me that Gulshan had woken up around 7.00 a.m. and had called him to say that at 8 he was going to meet a singer; at 8.30 he was supposed to meet a friend, after which he would go to the temple and then come to meet him.

When someone dies a violent unexpected death, people have a habit of recounting every moment of his before he died.

While he was talking, since I have this tendency all the time of thinking cinematically, I wondered, 'If Gulshan Kumar woke up at 7 o'clock, then at what time would the killer have woken up? Did he tell his mom to wake him up because he had a shooting to carry out? Did he have his breakfast before committing the crime or after?' These thoughts were coming into my head because I was trying to intercut the moments of the man who died with those of the man who killed him. Then it suddenly struck me that you always hear about gangsters only when they either kill or die. But what do they do in between? That was the thought which eventually resulted in *Satya*.

While in that frame of mind, I saw some photographs in *The Times of India* of arrested gangsters with black cloths covering their heads. Their body language did not betray any of the larger-than-life villainous characteristics they were shown to possess in Bollywood films. They looked very ordinary, guy-next-door kind of people. The whole point is that an urban gangster has to mix with society and look like anybody else so that you will not realize that he is a gangster.

A few days later a friend of mine, not a film guy, who lives on the fourteenth floor in Oshiwara, told me about an experience. A guy lived in his building somewhere in a flat above him. My friend used to bump into this guy in the building's lift once in a while. And they used to exchange the 'Hello, how are you?' 'Happy Diwali' kind of pleasantries. Then one day, my friend's wife told him that that guy had been arrested and taken away as he had been absconding in a murder case. My friend told me, 'The thing about Mumbai is that you may live for ten years as a neighbour to somebody and yet have no idea who he is.' That was how I got the plot line for *Satya:* the fact that Urmila's character lives in a chawl and Satya lives right next to her, yet she has no clue that he is a gangster.

Then one day, I met this guy called Ajit Devani who had been Mandakini's secretary and because of her one-time liaison with Dawood, he had reportedly known and interacted with some of the gangsters belonging to the Dawood Ibrahim–Chota Rajan gang when they were still together. He recounted to me an experience he had when he met a gangster whose brother had just been killed by the cops. His brother had also been a gangster. When Ajit Devani went to meet him, apparently the gangster was abusing his brother's dead body for not heeding his advice, resulting in his death. That startled me as I have never heard of a person abusing a dead body. Then I thought to myself that a gangster lives on power and the brother by not listening to his advice and getting himself killed, had taken away his power to save him and that's what brought on his anger. It was his grief which manifested as anger. I took that as the soul of Manoj Bajpayee's Bhiku Mhatre character and the incident inspired the scene where Bhiku Mhatre abuses Chander after his death.

We are social beings. We say 'Good morning', 'Hello, how are you' when greeting someone and that's what we call civilized. I thought an anti-social element lives by his own rules and he would not abide by the social rules and norms. The way he sits on a chair, the way he laughs, his general behaviour would have a certain wildness about it. There is a difference in look between a domestic cat and a wildcat; it's the eyes that give away the difference. I felt Bhiku Mhatre should be like a wildcat. I thought that if Bhiku Mhatre had gone to school, he would have been one of the last benchers and he wouldn't have taken his studies or any kind of advice seriously. So he would want to be a law unto himself.

I went to check out a beer bar in Borivali, whose owner was supposedly connected to the underworld, for a location. When I walked into his room, I was startled to see a huge amount of cash lying on the mat in plain sight. As I tried to persuade him to let me use his location, just the sight of all that money lying around made me feel very uneasy. After I came out, I wondered why the sight of that money had made me feel uneasy. After some thought I figured out that it's a normal reaction to hide the valuables when a stranger comes visiting, but by not hiding the money the beer bar owner was sending a subconscious or conscious signal to me that he didn't need to be scared of anyone because of who he was.

Then later on when I met him while I was shooting in that area, he was very friendly; he looked like a different person altogether. Then I realized that the first time I met him, he was trying to play up to an image which he thought I had of him. I know many celebrities who do that…if celebs think that anyone thinks very highly of them, then their body language changes. That is what this gangster was doing. Obviously when you're putting on an act, you can't sustain it for a long period of time. So after some time, he became normal. This is what I used for Kallu Mama's character in *Satya*. When the builder comes to meet him, Kallu Mama pretends he is a heavyweight gangster when he is actually the clown in the gang, which people come to know later. Since the builder was coming in awe of meeting a dangerous gangster, he created an image to cater to his expectations.

So each and every character in *Satya* was modelled on some gangster I had met or some gangster I had heard of, or sometimes on people I knew, not necessarily from the underworld. All in all, every character in *Satya* had a reference point.

But the chief protagonist's character was the most unclear in my head. He was unclear to me till even after the shooting. I was confused between whether he had a criminal streak or he was just a normal guy who became that way.

Once I decided that this was the kind of film I wanted to make, the first person who came to meet me as a writer was Anurag Kashyap. I took him on board and he got in Saurabh Shukla. We had a lot of discussion, but I wasn't able to clearly make up my mind what exactly to do in the film. So there was no concrete script on the day we started shooting. I went by instinct. The advantage was that I didn't have stars, so all the actors were available all the time.

In the first scene I was shooting, a goon played by Sushant

comes to Satya for hafta and Satya slashes his face with a knife. In my mind I had planned that would be the point at which to cut the shot. Sushant was someone my assistant had got and I didn't even know he was an actor, just a junior artiste. But since Sushant is a good actor, he improvised and after Satya slashed him before I could say 'cut', he screamed in pain. His scream startled me because I wasn't expecting him to so I forgot to say 'cut'. Because I didn't say 'cut', this guy who was showing him the koli improvised, saying, '*Oh ho, paani lao, paani lao*.' So the scene went on beyond its original conception because I didn't say cut and because the actors improvised. That is when it finally struck me how *Satya* should be made.

While capturing a scene, most directors have a tendency to pre-decide how it should start and how it should end. I decided to make *Satya* around the actual content conceived by me—in the style of what happened before and what after. All the realistic performances happened because I didn't restrict actors to a script. I just wanted them to improvise whatever they felt like. Actors were instructed not to follow written lines but just say whatever they felt like. So most of the time they were told the content and they kept improvising, and I controlled the lags in the editing.

The interesting thing to note here is that *Satya*'s unusual style came about largely due to Sushant's unexpected scream.

If he had not screamed or if I had told him before itself that the shot would be cut on the slash, *Satya* wouldn't have been the same.

Like I said I didn't have a clear story. I kept on changing my mind everyday about the storyline, but I was very clear about the characters. Where Satya's character is concerned, however, things went wrong compared to everyone else because of my own lack of clarity about the story and hence about the main protagonist. So I kept on changing the character to suit the plot line, whereas Bhiku Mhatre, Kallu Mama, Muley, and so on could all be consistent because there was nothing for them in the main plot of the film, which was primarily about the growth and decline of Satya. Satya slashes someone in cold blood in one scene and in another shyly smiles at Bhiku Mhatre after killing Jaggu, and when Bhiku Mhatre is having a fight with his wife, Satya stares at them like a zombie. Why did he do that? He did that because I told him to. The inconsistency relatively disconnected him from the audience compared to the other characters.

Company

I happened to meet a guy called Haneef at a producer's house. Haneef had been in jail in the serial blasts case for five years and was very close to Dawood Ibrahim.

Out of curiosity and my obsession with the criminal psyche, I got talking to him. In about an hour that I spent in Haneef's company, he told me various things about how the underworld operates. Those were also the days where the media was full of stories of the war between Dawood and Chota Rajan, and in that context he said, 'So many people on both sides have died in their war with each other. They so desperately want to kill each other, but Ramuji I am telling you this, even today if Dawood calls Rajan on the phone, if Rajan is smoking a cigarette he will drop it and say, "Haan! Dawood Bhai!" That is the inherent respect he has for Dawood. They hate each other because they love each other.' These lines by Haneef gave me the idea for *Company*.

Also in my research for *Satya*, there were so many things I learnt about the underworld which I could not incorporate in one film, especially the police procedures.

So if Haneef's take on the Dawood and Chota Rajan war gave me the story, my research gave me the atmosphere; the supporting characters and incidents I have more or less drawn from experiences with the staff in my own production company over the years. The reason for this is that I always found a very strong resemblance between the rivalries and internal politics in the underworld and normal office politics and rivalries, because human nature is the same everywhere. The people who work in any company have their own individualities and intelligence levels and the only thing common among them is the ambition and greed to reach the top. So even though the company as whole is working towards a goal, the personal ambitions will conflict with each other, creating politics, frustration, jealousy, etc.

While this is true of any company, whether normal or underworld, the difference is that in a normal company if you make a mistake you will be fired and in an underworld company you will be fired at.

Bad company

I want to share an interesting aspect of *Company*'s prologue where eagles are flying over the city. Much after the main shoot of the film was over, I asked my cameraman to take some shots of the city to use them in the edit and, while he was doing that, the eagles just happened to be there at one location and he shot them flying around. When I saw the rushes on Avid, those shots reminded me of the opening scene of *Mackenna's Gold*, one of my all-time favourite films, and I was seized by a desire to somehow incorporate them in the film. My editor suggested that he could use them for exterior cuts of the city at various places in between the film. I felt that would just make it informative, whereas I wanted it to create drama like in *Mackenna's Gold*.

So I thought of using them with a profound-sounding voiceover. I wrote the line 'Eagles have a lot of patience and they wait for months to get to their prey.' My assistant told me eagles didn't do that. So I changed it to 'Very few people know that eagles have lot of patience and they wait for months to get to their prey.'

I told my assistant that most of the people sitting in the theatre wouldn't know anything about eagles anyway, and the fact that we were saying that very few people knew it, would make each of them feel that they were among the many who didn't know this fact of natural history. Even if a few didn't buy it, by the end of the film they would take it for granted that it was not to be taken literally.

Even today, thirteen years after I made the film, people talk to me about the effect of that prologue and only I know in my heart it came from nothing more profound than a childish desire of mine to somehow use that *Mackenna's Gold*-like shot in the film.

The 'Khallas' song in the film is another thing that people remember. I did unique experimentation in it. I told the choreographer that we wouldn't give any objective space to the camera, and would treat it as one of the guests in the club. Typically in a song shoot, we have the frame designed for the camera and everything is placed and moved according to its convenience but the moment we took that away and created a subjective space, a kind of unpredictability came in. I told the cameraman to keep zooming and panning to whatever attracted him as an individual irrespective of what the choreographer or I had to say. Lastly, I told the editor to edit it so as to evoke hazy recollections, half-dreamy and half-real, that one has in the morning after staying late at a night club and passing out once one is back home. After this brief to the three, I pretty much stayed out of both the shoot and the edit. The efforts of three superb technicians in keeping with their individual briefing and my effort to see that they didn't coordinate with each other is what resulted in 'Khallas'.

When people ask me which is my favourite of the two, *Satya* or *Company*, I find it very difficult to answer as the difference between them is that *Satya* is emotional and *Company* is intelligent. Depending on my state of mind then, I alternate between the two.

Incidentally Haneef, who gave me the idea for *Company*, was shot dead a few months after I met him, and the last thing he told me or rather advised me when he got to know I was making *Company* was not to waste my time doing dark films and instead make a romantic musical. Maybe he was bad company but he certainly gave me good *Company*.

Chapter 26

Making of Aag: 'Bahut Lambi Kahani Hai Yeh'

THE IDEA OF DOING something with *Sholay* came around five-six years ago, when one day I got a call from Sasha Sippy saying that his grandfather Mr G.P. Sippy wanted to meet me. As he is a respected senior member of the fraternity as well as the producer of *Sholay*, I went all the way to town to meet him.

There Sasha Sippy mentioned that they were interested in making a sequel to *Sholay*. He already had a storyline worked out which revolved around Babban or 'Junior Gabbar', the son Helen bears Gabbar Singh after he sleeps with her post the 'Mehbooba' song.

The big problem with making a sequel to *Sholay* was that some of the characters had been killed off in the film and some of the actual cast had died. One of the central characters Jai, played by Amitabh Bachchan, had died in the film and Sanjeev Kumar and Amjad Khan had passed away in the real world. Therefore, one had to make do with the remaining characters and cast, and possibly create new characters.

According to Sasha's story Helen's son wanted revenge for his father Gabbar Singh, who was behind bars because of Jai and Veeru. Veeru and Basanti visited Ramgarh village now and then to meet Radha, who was still residing in the village. They were kidnapped by Junior Gabbar. Then both Veeru and Basanti's sons come to the rescue. This was the basic plot line Sasha had in mind.

In this plot, he wanted me to weave in a part for Jackie Chan. I first thought he meant some local actor named Jackie Chan, till I realized that he was talking about the Hong Kong superstar. Sasha Sippy's Jackie Chan brainwave was owing to the runaway success of *Rush Hour* where an American and an Asian actor were teamed together. I found the whole thing so bizarre that I politely declined the offer and came away laughing. Little did I realize that the last laugh would be on me…!

Kya Socha, Kya Nikla?

Anyway, cutting again to the flashback, on my way back from the meeting with the Sippys, it suddenly occurred to me that if the story of *Sholay* was set in contemporary times in a city, it might be interesting. I bounced it off some people around me and they all thought it a splendid idea.

Then just for the heck of it, I started effecting simple changes such as instead of Gabbar's famous '*Kitne admi the?*' he should say '*Kitne*'. I thought if Sanjeev Kumar didn't have hands how could he have shaved everyday? So let's have Thakur with a beard. So I basically went on this trip of literally interpreting shots and dialogues and scenes, and completely forgot the basic emotional connect of the film, which was the only thing that would have made a sequel work.

When I was disssecting each of the shots and scenes, people around me also came under the spell and I started thinking that maybe over the years *Sholay* had completely broken up into audio-visual bytes. You still remembered lines from it, made caricaturish characters from it and remembered particular scenes and shots. So it was kind of fragmented into parts and you didn't look at it as a whole film experience, and that's how it became at least in my mind.

I psyched the people around me also into thinking that way. I know it sounds stupid, it sounds stupid to me too now. I made a few people sit and started talking about for example Amitabh Bachchan's character. In Gabbar's introduction, I told them he would be drunk with power, hence have a laidback stance. And he would have a characteristic laughter sounding like a cough. Everybody around me thought it a fantastic interpretation.

When the film was released, someone came up to me and told me Gabbar looked like he had fever in his introductory scene in the film as he is coughing. Now if one looks at it from that point of view, yes it sounds like he has fever. So everything I thought so seriously about turned out seriously wrong.

One day as I was sitting around with four-five people, a commercial poster designer came to me with a poster design of Gabbar. My first instinct was 'Why would any city dweller wear such clothes' because my idea at that point of time was still to make it very realistic but the people around me said it was fantastic.

When I said that it didn't look real, the designer said, 'In the old *Sholay*, Gabbar was a normal guy but over the years he has become a legend. So Gabbar should not look realistic, he should look very stylized.' Everyone said he was right. Now the point is that they didn't know what I had in mind. I was very clear about what I wanted, but just under the influence of that particular moment with so many people seemingly excited about it, I thought that maybe I was missing something, maybe he was right in what he meant by legend. So I decided not to get stuck to my original thought and be flexible.

Then I took it over to Amitji, and he also said it was

fantastic. But Amitji also didn't know what I had in mind. He took it for granted, the professional that he is, that I knew what I was doing. And he had developed so much of trust in me as a director post *Sarkar*, he thought I must be having some reason behind designing such a look. Seeing that Amitabh Bachchan also thought it fantastic and other people around also found it fantastic, I put down my own resistance to a mental block.

Then with that look as reference point, I started changing the look of each of the characters and situations, what kind of a place he would stay in, etc. ... I just got completely carried away by the technical aspect of trying to match up to this design which somebody else had given. I tried to match everything to that look and obviously couldn't because the scenes and characters and emotions were at loggerheads. So I started manipulating things or psyching myself and whoever was there. Each of the actors, whether Ajay Devgn, Sushmita Sen, Mohanlal, Amitabh Bachchan, Nisha Kothari or Prashant Raj, was completely convinced the film was heading in the right direction primarily because of my psyching. So they were also not able to look at the film in totality. Also, by that time, the hype around my remaking *Sholay* was so much, it was almost impossible for me to detach and take a fresh look at it.

To complicate things further, initially the lawyers told me that there was no copyright problem, and I didn't need to take rights because of my completely fresh interpretation. After I started, they said you can't do this and you have to change this character, you cannot have these many scenes in a sequence, so I kept changing scenes and characters. It is very dangerous to start changing scenes once you start a film because you don't know what is going to be affected in the final cut.

I could not get the title *Sholay*, so like *Ram Gopal Varma's Sarkar* or *Sanjay Leela Bhansali's Devdas*, I settled on *Ram Gopal Varma ki Sholay*. Then, by the time it was released, the court gave an order not to use the word 'sholay'. I had no choice but to substitute it with something that had a meaning close to sholay. So we just chucked out 'sholay' and bunged in 'aag' and *Ram Gopal Varma ki Sholay* became *Ram Gopal Varma ki Aag*. In short, whatever *could* go wrong, went wrong, with *Aag*.

But all these are still minor hazards of being a filmmaker, compared to the dangers of a being surrounded by people who will not tell one the truth. It is not that they necessarily mean to cause any harm, but they may just not want to be contrarian or may be afraid or psyched or may just, mistakenly, believe that the filmmaker is always moving to plan.

It also came as a shock to me that most people in the twelve to thirty age group hadn't seen *Sholay*. So they couldn't make head or tail of *Aag*, which was a stylized interpretation premised on the notion that the audience had all seen the original orthodox version. As for the people who remembered the original *Sholay,* they didn't like the intrusion of new characters and the new way of telling the story. So, to all of them, *Aag* looked like a ridiculous collage of scenes going nowhere and it became one of the biggest disasters of Indian cinema.

When people ask me if I was hurt by the brickbats, I must say I wasn't, because I learnt a lot from the experience and I truly believe that I am a better director today because of *Aag*. Yes, I do feel terribly guilty because I made so many people, actors, technicians and investors party to a blunder I was single-handedly responsible for—from my preposterous rehash of the dialogues to going against my gut feeling about Gabbar's look and the ridiculous title. They put in their time, money and hard work and trusted my vision and suffered the consequences for no fault of theirs.

But one thing about *Aag* that makes me happy is that the film did manage to provide mass entertainment if only in ripping it apart. The one thing I regret most about *Aag* is that, being the butt of it, I was the only one who didn't get to f**k it.

Chapter 27

It was Sex That Made Sarkar Happen

I WAS IN MY senior inter when a friend of mine gave me a book called *The Godfather*, telling me to enjoy the explicit sex scene on page 26. I ran back home and after devouring the vivid description of Sonny having sex with his girlfriend in the privacy of my room, I idly turned to the back cover and the blurb said something about the Mafia, a word I had never come across before. Having nothing better to do, I started reading the book. The narrative, the characters and the drama had me so utterly riveted that I think I read the book three to four times, almost back to back.

Every time I finished reading it I started rereading and

every time I read it, I discovered fresh nuances and minute details. Its effect on me was so profound that it got me hooked to reading fiction, and I would say my interest in wanting to be a storyteller through films started primarily from there. And so *The Godfather* and my interest in novels came about only because of my adolescent urgings. Long after that when I became a director, I often used *The Godfather* as reference—the scenes, the dialogue delivery or some moment from here and there. For example, in *Satya* there is the voiceover describing the aftermath of Amodh Shukla's murder. That was directly lifted from Mario Puzo's description of the aftermath of Sollozzo's killing. *Shiva* too had its *The Godfather* moments. But the idea of fully adapting the novel took shape only in 2002, and I immediately approached Amitabh Bachchan with it.

In spite of many people not having heard of the Mafia as it is an Italian/American phenomenon, *The Godfather* has such resonance across the world because people who can influence others with the strength of their personalities and their tremendous power exist everywhere in the form of ganglords, political leaders, dictators or kings.

In the Indian context, I thought the closest anybody came to the Don was Balasaheb Thackeray—a man without any official position or political seat who could, just out of his sheer personal charisma, affect people so profoundly that they were willing to die and kill for him. So I used him as reference point in *Sarkar*, my loose adaptation of *The Godfather*. I would say that the primary difference between *Sarkar* and *The Godfather* film is not the Indian versus American setting, but that my film is influenced more by the book than the film version. I was deeply impressed with the certain mythological larger-than-life quality that the book has but I think the film lacks.

There is a line in the book, 'From 1935 to 1937 the name of Santino Corleone sent shockwaves through the underworld.' James Caan playing the role of Santino Corleone did not bring this line alive for me, but Kay Kay Menon who plays Vishnu Nagre does. That is what I mean by taking reference from the tone of the book. Likewise, in the beginning when Amerigo Bonasera talks to the Don to help him bring the people who hurt his daughter to justice, I found the conversation a bit unreal—'How much do you want? Why did you do this to me? Why didn't you come to me first, instead of going to the police?' I felt it was unreal because these big people who have reached a certain status, go out of their way to help people in trouble, who come to them, in order to make them feel emotionally obligated. That is how they get to be so powerful, to have people willing to die for them. That thought also I took from the novel. In the opening scene of *Sarkar* when a guy gets out of a rickshaw and enters the gate of Sarkar's bungalow, you can see the defeat in his walk and hear it in his voice when he is talking to Sarkar about the injustice he's suffered. There you get sucked into Sarkar's state of mind and you feel the anger as much as him, whereas in *The Godfather* you look at the scene objectively.

My intention was also to make the audience feel intimidated by the characters. So all of them were introduced with a full-piece orchestra background score. For example, the way Rashid enters the house, the gate opening, the background score and the way he gets down from the car and goes up the staircase is almost like a Mahabharata character. So by the time he reaches Sarkar, the background score and the shots are commanding the audience to take him very seriously. This is accentuated by his sitting in front of Sarkar, taking his own time and seemingly not concerned or bothered or intimidated by Sarkar's stature. At a subconscious level, the audience also feels the impact of a new actor sitting in front of Amitabh Bachchan and not feeling intimidated.

When people ask me about my obsession with casting new actors, I feel it works because people have never seen that guy before and have no expectations of him. It allows me to play around with the audience's imagination. If I take a big name like Danny Denzongpa or Amrish Puri in an effort to match somebody with Amitabh Bachchan, I don't think a scene is effective enough because subconsciously the audience will anticipate the final outcome thereby making it predictable. With a new guy, they don't know what to make of him—how big he is, what he can do, how he can react. I think that unpredictability of an unknown face works very well in films of this genre. Abhishek's character, I initially imagined as a guy who's just a chilled-out boy and he becomes a man in the course of the film. But later I thought that right from the beginning I should make him larger than life. There is obviously some special quality in him that allows him to become what he does. He does not do what his father does or may not agree with it or he may not be so much into it, but that does not mean Shankar's larger-than-life quality shouldn't be apparent right from the time he comes out of the airport and in the way he walks. It is what I more or less maintain with all the characters in the film.

My tendency is to have a very dramatic and in-your-face background score. I have two reasons for this; one is that I find background score drives the emotion of the audience in a specified intended direction. At times people complain that it is so loud that one cannot hear the dialogue properly. Sometimes the reason for this is that by the time I reach the mixing stage, I am so bored of the dialogues myself, having heard them so many times before, that I feel like drowning them out in music. I know it sounds stupid but it can happen. So I think sometimes, if the body language of the characters and the build-up are able to convey the sense of the scene, it might be more effective to have the dialogues in the background and the music loud and foregrounded.

My favourite shot in *Sarkar* is in the end after the whole thing is resolved. This shot has Sarkar in the background waving to the crowd and as he turns back and walks, we hear someone speaking, and then Tanisha comes in and for a second you feel Tanisha is talking. Then as the camera moves back we see the silhouette of a woman talking to someone about her problem and as it pans, you see Shankar. This silhouette of the woman and Shankar, with Sarkar centrestage, conveys several things in a single shot: for the public Sarkar is still the boss and that's the way Shankar wants to keep it, not really wanting the credit for the work he's doing in the background; but the transition to his taking over has begun. It's not that the audience will consciously understand all that the scene is meant to convey, but it will feel the overall impact. I don't think the craft of cinema is so much about the audience consciously understanding but it has to feel the impact.

During the making of *Sarkar,* Abhishek and I often discussed the possibility of a sequel. *Sarkar* is basically about character conflicts. Obviously there are so many situations that occur in Sarkar's life. If he dealt with one such situation and one set of antagonists in *Sarkar,* then you could scale it up further and create another situation in the sequel.

Looking back, I felt *Sarkar* was a very simplistic story. It was so because it was based on the original *The Godfather* plot.

So many films have been made on that storyline, but it was just the newness of the meeting and the performances which made *Sarkar* stand apart. The sequel, I thought no longer had the freshness of the first to cash in on. But I couldn't change the style because that was the tradition of *Sarkar*. What I could do was to put in a story which was very original and make it on a scale and on issues which were bigger; I thought this would make it a lot more interesting than the first *Sarkar*.

What I felt when I saw *The Godfather: Part II* was that the characters were taken for granted. There was no intention on the part of the director to make them look larger than life, the way it was done in the first part. So I was somehow disappointed to see Michael Corleone running here and there. No doubt it is a great film and I have seen it many times, but I didn't want the intensity and larger-than-life quality of Sarkar to be diluted in *Sarkar Raj*. So in fact, I worked more than in *Sarkar* to sustain the larger-than-life treatment in terms of character portrayals. In spite of employing technological advancements of the last few years, I tried to stick to the tradition of *Sarkar.* Every technique was employed only to heighten the intensity of the actors, because I don't believe anything is bigger than an actor's performance and any time technology becomes central, a film will falter.

To sum up, on page 26 of *The Godfather* when Sonny's girlfriend said 'she felt something burning between her thighs', it amounted to something burning between my ears, and it kicked off my journey to becoming a filmmaker; though admittedly not on first reading, when it evoked very different feelings.

Chapter 28

Munna's Yellow Outfit

IN MY COLLEGE I used to hang out with a street goonda called Ramesh. Those days it was pretty common for students to be interacting with goonda elements. Ramesh was a much feared guy in the locality, and my friends and I held him in awe. We spent endless hours with him at an Irani hotel.

He developed a huge crush on one of the college girls, which slowly turned into serious love on his part. But he always looked at her from afar and refused to talk to her in spite of our encouragement. I thought it pretty ironical that such a tough guy would turn so tender when it came to her.

He always wore dirty chappals, but one day came wearing a brand new pair of Nike shoes. They looked so funny on him that everyone made fun of him. He was hurt and I could see that it was his attempt at smartening himself up to impress the girl.

The girl started seeing this rich, good-looking guy who was one of the very few people in those days with a car of his own. All of us chamchas started goading Ramesh to go beat up the guy and get him out of the way. Ramesh turned around and in a choked voice said that she deserved the best and the other guy was better suited to her in every way. Rangeela took birth at that moment in that Irani café. The Nike shoes incident would appear in the film as Munna wearing the yellow outfit.

I had heard stories of how Sridevi's mother used to be a junior artiste, and how she would go from studio to studio to make her daughter a star. I kind of combined both her and her daughter into one and created the character of Mili.

I based Jackie Shroff's character on the Countess in *The Sound of Music*. I liked the dignity with which the character was treated, resisting the temptation of depicting her as a vamp. Once I finished the story, I wanted to make it in Telugu with Sridevi and Nagarjuna and was planning to ask Rajinikanth to make a guest appearance. However, both Sridevi and Nagarjuna did not like the story. They chose instead the story of *Govindha Govindha*. Primarily, I think, not so much because of the concept itself, but more because they thought I would be better in action films because of my *Shiva* background. So I kind of forgot about the subject for a few years.

Meanwhile, at some point I came to Mumbai to sign up Madhuri Dixit for a role opposite Nagarjuna for my film *Antham* (*Drohi*). Madhuri had no dates available and Boney Kapoor suggested this new girl called Urmila, who had acted in a film called *Narasimha*. I wasn't particularly impressed with her but, because there was no time and no one else available, I signed her up. Neither the film nor she worked. A few months later Mani Ratnam and I worked together on a script called *Gaayam*, in which Revathi was the main lead and for a supporting role Mani suggested Urmila, not because he thought her a great new talent but because he thought she would work in that role.

I was planning to shoot a song with Urmila for *Gaayam* in Vizag when a choreographer called Suchitra missed her train to Vizag. So instead of cancelling the shoot, I asked Urmila if she could dance to the music by herself, which she did. I was mesmerized and decided to cast her in *Rangeela* there and then.

I loved Aamir in *Qayamat Se Qayamat Tak* and *Raakh*. I used to meet him off and on in Mumbai. He loved my first film *Shiva* and we were planning to work together. I went to meet him with the *Rangeela* script and he liked it immediately.

I happened to see Mani Ratnam's *Roja* songs which really blew me away; for the first time in my career they inspired me with a desire to shoot songs aesthetically. So I went about seeing all the great Hollywood musicals, in the course of which I observed that my mother was not flinching in the *Singin' in the Rain* song sequences even though there was so much exposure of the girls' bodies in them. She was otherwise conservative and strongly disapproved of the 'Sarkai Lo Khatiya' David Dhawan–Karishma kind of songs. Then I realized it was *how* they were made to expose not *how much* that mattered. In Indian films at that time, girls were made to feel crass and dirty while exposing and so a hardness would come on their faces. The *Singin' in the Rain* girls on the other hand were exposing with a sense of pride in their bodies and a feeling of joy. In both cases, my mother was connecting to the feeling and not to the bodies. So I told Urmila, 'If you feel beautiful, you will come across as beautiful and if you feel that you are doing something vulgar, that's how you will come across.'

I wanted the songs to be visually very appealing and 'Hai Rama' to be extremely erotic with Jackie's and Urmila's eyes showing lust rather than romance. I thought animals don't hide behind closed walls or look for a dark place to make love. When they are in the mood for it, they do it in broad daylight anywhere, any place and nothing matters but their desire for each other. You see that in the sequence in 'Hai Rama' when Urmila and Jackie are circling each other in the Kuldhara ruins with lust in their eyes.

Somewhere halfway through the film, Aamir started having doubts about the script, and with valid reason. He said if

Munna was an extrovert, sold tickets in black and had such a flamboyant personality, why would he delay telling Mili that he loved her. He felt that just for the convenience of the screenplay I was delaying that aspect. Put that way, he was absolutely right, but I thought nobody had felt it when I was narrating the story, including Aamir, which meant the emotional drama was carrying it forward; now, since Aamir had had time to think, he saw it as a problem.

He also felt if Mili was a nice girl, Munna a nice guy and Jackie also a nice guy, there was absolutely no drama anywhere, and the whole film was resting on just that one element of Munna not telling Mili till the end.

However, he told me that as no two people can have the same vision and since I was the director, he would go along with my vision in spite of disagreeing with it. Contrary to popular perception, Aamir is an absolutely non-interfering actor to work with. He is a very intelligent man, with tremendous sincerity, and wants to make sure that the film holds together logically. But since most people, including myself, don't have his sincerity, our guilt makes us say that he interferes; for the record, though, I have never said it.

When the film became a big hit, Aamir hugged me and said that he was glad to have been proved wrong. But that is not necessarily true. Maybe the film would have been a much bigger hit if I had incorporated his suggestions. Also, in my heart I knew that if the film hadn't worked, it would have been for precisely the fears Aamir had raised.

Anyway the much-publicized controversy between Aamir and me happened six to seven months after *Rangeela* was released. Khalid Mohamed was doing an interview with me in which I was explaining that the audience can rarely understand the difference between a character and an actor. I cited the scene in *Rangeela* when Aamir takes Urmila to a restaurant. The waiter, being a five-star hotel steward, is higher in social status than Munna, but being a waiter he has no choice but to serve him. At a human level, though, he can barely hide his disgust on hearing Munna's lines. I told Khalid that the lines are being delivered by Aamir but the look on the waiter's face is what is making the audience laugh. So it calls for more complex acting on the waiter's part compared to Aamir in that particular scene. Khalid, who apparently had a personal axe to grind with Aamir, made it sound in the article like I'd said the waiter was a better actor than Aamir. By the time the article came out, I was in interior Andhra Pradesh on a Telugu film shoot, and as there were no cell phones those days Aamir couldn't contact me. Seeing that I was not getting in touch with him and not knowing where I was, Aamir thought I was avoiding him. As the media was hounding him to react, he went ahead and reacted, and the media blew the thing up into a full-scale war. The moment I realized what had happened, I met Aamir and explained things to him. He wanted me to give a statement in print against Khalid that I had been misquoted. I said I couldn't because I *had* said all those things, only they were quoted out of context to make them sound different from the way they were meant. It was my mistake to have spoken to Khalid about something that was too technical for a layperson to understand.

Some cold vibes still remained between us, with good reason, till years later we met at a party and had a long chat; since then we are on cordial terms again. Whatever happened between Aamir and me was completely my fault, and I am saying this here now, because I haven't trusted any journalist to put it across in the correct perspective until now.

Chapter 29

The Biggest Flop of My Life

SOMETIME IN 1994, I had just returned to Hyderabad from Chennai in the morning and was supposed to catch an evening flight to Mumbai. I was taking a nap in the afternoon when my sister suddenly woke me up and told me my distant cousin Bujji from Bhimavaram was on the phone. (Those days there were no cell phones.) I wondered why she had woken me up for that, and she said Bujji had said it was very urgent. Curious, as Bujji was not even that close to me, I went to the phone and Bujji said that dad had had a heart attack and died, and before I could say anything, he asked me if I was alone. When I said 'no' as my mom and sister were around, he asked me to go out and call him from a public phone. I walked to an STD booth at the end of the road with my brother-in-law following me. I was wondering why Bujji was being so secretive about his dad dying of a heart attack. As I was nearing the booth, it slowly dawned upon me that he was talking about my dad. I turned around and asked my brother-in-law where my dad was, and he said he had gone to Bhimavaram the previous day.

I called up Bujji and he confirmed my fear, and asked me whether we would be coming there or if he should bring the body to Hyderabad. I told him to bring the body. I turned around and told my brother-in-law what had happened, and he just sat down on the road in shock. I personally was not feeling anything as I was concentrating on how to break the news to my mother. I quickly made a few calls to some relatives and told them that they would get to hear it from somewhere sooner or later and asked them not to come to the house till I had prepared my mother.

Walking back, I thought of a story to tell my mother. I told her that dad had suffered some pain in the chest, and I had asked them to bring him to Hyderabad as there were better medical facilities there. When she got panicky, I told her cheerfully that he was perfectly fine. My intention was to reduce the time of her grief before the body reached, and also to have time to plan how to make her slowly absorb the final shock. I literally went about doing a screenplay of sorts, sent some guys to the end of the road to stop any overenthusiastic relatives coming over to console her, and made a friend of mine do mock phone conversations in front of my mother as if he was talking to people who were bringing back my father and to say that the pain was increasing. That was my way of slowly breaking the news to my mother.

This whole charade went on till 11 p.m. and then I went off to sleep. So far I had not felt anything at all as I was too busy directing scenes to cushion my mother. At around 2 a.m., my cousin woke me up and said the body had arrived. I came out and saw the car in which they brought the body on the road, and that's when it first hit me. I told my cousin to take the car to his house and only bring it in the morning so that we could quickly arrange the cremation and spare my mother the trauma of sitting up with the body till morning. Around 5 a.m., my grandfather broke the news to my mother and by that time, seeing all the activity building up, I am sure she already suspected it.

My uncle came and told me that my father had written a will wanting to donate his eyes and body. My relatives told me to ignore the will and perform the rites as per tradition. I said I wanted to respect my father's wishes, and went and asked my mother if she would have any objection to my going by dad's wishes. She asked me to do whatever I thought was right, even though she was weeping. I called the eye institute guys and two young nurses landed up in a rickshaw. I still remember them laughing as they got out of the rickshaw at some private joke between them. Their cheerful laughter contrasted so macabrely with the crying and the sombre atmosphere. They sent everyone out, took out the eyes and after they left my people told me it was time to take the body to hospital. I went in to see my mother next to the body of my father, and there was a redness around his eyes and a slit which was angled because of whatever the girls from the institute did to take out the eyes.

I felt very guilty and angry with myself for having subjected my mother to seeing the man she had lived with for forty years that way for the last time, especially since she always used to say how much she loved my father's eyes. In the name of fulfilling my father's wishes, I had failed to foresee the pain my decision would subject my mother to. I rate this as the biggest flop of my life.

Next day, I told my mother that we should avoid any seventh- or eleventh-day kind of rituals as we should remember him from happy times and not make an exhibition seeking sympathy. I gave her a long lecture on how she should look at everything positively. The next day I heard my mother crying in her room and was upset that my lecture hadn't worked. In the afternoon, I heard a strange sound and found my brother crying upstairs. That was the first time I had ever heard him cry and I was thinking to myself that this was how it sounded when he cried. Throughout this period I did not for one second feel any grief myself, and that had nothing to do with my relationship with my father. I loved and respected him immensely. It's just that I was in a state of film, for want of a better term.

I went to Mumbai a few days later to meet Naseeruddin Shah as I was casting him in a film. As soon as he saw me he got up and said he was very sorry to hear about my mother. Somebody had given him wrong information that it was my mother who had died, and so as not to embarrass him, I didn't correct him. Then he went on to talk about his mother and asked how my father was taking it. The fact that I hadn't corrected him right in the beginning made it even more difficult now to tell him that he'd got it wrong. So I went on with the charade.

Years later, somewhere in 2003 or so, I was in Pune at Nana Patekar's house. Nana, Shimit Amin, Sandeep Srivastava (the writer of *Ab Tak Chhappan*) and I were doing a script session. In the context of a scene, as a reference I started narrating the episode of my father's death, and when I came to the part about the nurses from the eye institute and its aftermath, I suddenly choked and broke down. Nana had to hold me in his arms to control me. It took me nine years to cry and that too for more than my father; it was for that biggest flop I ever made.

CRITICS/THE MEDIA:
WHY I LOVE-HATE THEM

Chapter 30

I Love the Hate

SOMEONE SENT ME A review of a film I had made. I was thrilled to bits at the venom spewed by the critic. I just couldn't believe the amount of hatred he had developed for me through my films. The interesting thing is that he saw the film with much more intensity and seriousness than I made it with, and he saw it with the express purpose of hating it.

Similarly, on a visit to the film institute in Pune, where I was screening a film of mine, I was amazed to see the violent anger of one young student against me because of his hatred of the film. I was both amused and sorry.

I am fascinated to see how people run down films, critique them, ridicule them, bitch about them and sometimes also try to analyse the directors' minds through their films. It is so entertaining to see the critics' views and interpretations of our works. Everyone in the film fraternity will vouch for the fact that all critics, without exception, are wannabe filmmakers and that's why they hate filmmakers who are already where they themselves want to be.

I can understand them being bored by a film…but why hate? I don't buy the theory that it comes from expectations. I have made 'bad' films much more often in the last twenty years. It is not as if I have surprised anybody with a 'bad' film. The reverse is true; I have surprised people every once in a while with a 'good' film.

I feel these days media hatred is directed more at the director than at the film. If I make a bad film, they feel that I am getting away with murder. The anger in most cases seems to result from their frustration at not being able to find backers for their films whereas I, seemingly callous and dispassionate about my work and producing what they think is crap day after day, always have a long list of backers. Basically, it's the righteous anger of these 'honest, law-abiding' citizens against the success of others. Love and hate, I think, are extremely valuable emotions, and should not be wasted so facilely. It is more worthwhile to lean back and study what makes those people tick.

When I was looking for a break for my first film, I was trying to meet a producer who, in my view, was making crap films compared to my script. For hours, I used to stand outside while he was sitting with people I thought were worthless directors. But instead of getting frustrated and angry, I used that time to try and study him and the people around him, and devise plans for somehow making him see the wisdom of trusting me.

When someone is up there and he deserves to be up there, try to learn from what he has achieved. If you think he doesn't deserve it, still try to learn from what he has achieved and add your own capability to it, as it might result in you climbing higher than him. But you should not sit on the ground, gazing at him with hatred and waiting for him to fall, because his descent won't help you reach the top. And also you might often miss the point that people whom you look down upon may actually be far more capable than you. Anyway, to cut a long story short, I feel it's truly wasteful to expend your energy in hating someone. Love will at least, sometimes, give you good sex whereas hate will give you nothing.

If I have misread, misunderstood or misinterpreted your hatred, I apologize to all you critics, and you may consider this piece of writing just one more flop of mine.

I have no doubts that after reading this you will hate me more, but then don't forget that I will love you more!

Chapter 31

My Take on the Media

THE MEDIA IS A reporting agency. It reports news. News is something you hear for the first time, and for it to catch your attention, the media has to make the news sound as dramatic as possible. Television channels and newspapers have no choice but to do that so as to be able to stay in business and make money. So finally is it only about making money? Not necessarily; it could also be for individual egos and clamouring for fame among journalists. Most media people bitch about each other as much as they bitch about others. But again, like any other industry, you cannot generalize. Like there are good, bad and ugly filmmakers, there are good, bad and ugly journalists, but eventually they are all human.

The interesting thing is how smoothly and without anybody

consciously realizing it, the media has changed its role from news reporting to power-mongering and moneymaking.

What the media basically does is to strip everybody and make money out of it. The only difference between a stripteaser and the media is that a stripteaser bares herself to make money and the media strips others to make money.

Does anyone out there believe that anybody in the media truly feels the gravity or tragedy of the things they are reporting? They can hardly conceal their excitement when tragic things happen. The more horrific the better, as they will grab more eyeballs. Similarly, if someone famous trips up, they delight in it. Have you noticed the pleasure they get in ripping apart films or people's character? But the film people are worse.

For all the anger filmwallahs display against critics, it is actually they, excepting obviously the targets of the bitching and ripping, who enjoy and relish the nasty and bitchy comments or reviews much more than the public. The reason for this is nothing but jealousy and jealousy, is a human trait that like lots of other emotions gets magnified in the context of the entertainment industry.

The basic reason for jealousy is that people by nature cannot bear anyone else to be successful, and one way of feeling successful even if one has not achieved anything is to watch with glee someone else fail and be ripped to shreds, and the media supplies this pleasure to everyone. I think I truly deserve to be thanked for creating *Aag*. It has provided so much material to the media for dishing out entertainment to the public at large by ripping it apart. If entertainment is the sole purpose of a film, I think *Aag* has done more than its bit, definitely much more than it could have done in theatres even had it turned out a success.

The pressure to perform and fear of failure and ridicule are most heightened in the film industry and that is mainly because of the media. Nobody knows or is interested in what decisions went wrong in a hotelier's or a cloth merchant's business and how much money he lost, but if a filmmaker makes a flop, everybody will know of it because of the media. Fair enough, the media is also responsible for the fame a filmmaker achieves with a hit.

And *fame* is the key word here. Much more than money everybody wants fame; those who come to the industry want to develop their own identities. And media critics are equally desperate to have their individual fame and identities. As a consequence, they tend to love the way they rip the film apart much more than they hate the film.

A reporter's job is truly thankless, what with day after day, hour after hour, having to find something to report about. And so fierce is the competition that it has to be sensational enough to grab eyeballs at any cost. So much so, it is often even at the cost of hurting people, even those he knows on a personal level

(*Agar ghoda ghaas se dosti karega toh khaayega kya*?). When he gets a whiff of an interesting story on someone, a journalist's greatest fear is its denial by the person concerned. But the necessity of having to feed the media monster is so compelling that he will cook up something even in that situation.

Once a journo from *Mumbai Mirror* texted me to ask if there was a rift between Amitji and me, to which I replied in the negative. He sent the same message to Amitji, and Amitji replied that he was planning to do twenty films with me. One would imagine that he would have dropped the story at this point as the only two people who could confirm or deny it had categorically denied it. But he went ahead anyway and ran a story with the headline 'Kaput… Ramu and Bachchan relationship over'. He gave all kinds of reasons—what he had heard or imagined—and, incredibly, at the end quoted Amitji's and my denials in small print.

Now why would he do that? It was simply because he knew that most people read only the headlines and even if anybody reads the rest, they remember only the headlines, just as people always remember the number of stars a movie gets rather than the reviews.

The proof of this is the number of media people who asked me about the rift, taking their cue from that article. When I asked if they hadn't read the denials, they grudgingly admitted they had, almost as if given a choice they would rather believe the rift part of it than the denial, because the rift is news and it will help fill news columns, web-space and TV footage, whereas Amitji's and my closeness is a known fact and hence not newsworthy. So the long and short of it is, if so many media people and film industry people can have a field day discussing, speculating and getting entertained by the juicy piece of gossip, the irritation and pain it will cause to just two people, namely Amitji and me, can be ignored in the larger interest of making fools out of the common people.

Similarly, a report mentioning a war between Karan Johar and me appeared where the reporter claimed that I had lashed out at Karan in my blog. Now, even a dimwit could see that I was joking and making fun of everything and most of all myself in that blog post. It wasn't as if the reporter couldn't, but he chose not to as he wanted to use only what suited his own agenda.

Another interesting thing is the difference between the Mumbai media and the media elsewhere. It's primarily because most of the Mumbai media hobnobs and rubs shoulders with the film people.

The film people, out of fear and greed and in order to use the media, open their doors to journalists and almost become informants about their colleagues. So the media kind of loses its primary objective and tends to get embroiled in the camp culture of the industry, overstepping its reporting role.

When one journalist with a top newspaper that could reportedly influence awards wanted to use actors and technicians to make films, they all obliged, primarily out of fear of bad reviews and greed of awards. He openly used his position in the newspaper to write against people he wanted to settle personal scores with, and on top of that bragged about it to all and sundry.

Another journalist has the unique trait of calling up film folk whenever they are low after a failed project and soothing them and giving them a shoulder to cry on. He gives and takes information from various people and passes it on to the others concerned. Most in Bollywood trust him more than journalists who stay in Mumbai because he stays out of town and is just a voice on the phone. So they feel safer confiding in him as he is far away, and imagine that what they tell him won't circulate back.

The media elsewhere, since it does not have that much of access to film people, is relatively unbiased and has comparatively more integrity. Another big problem is that all of us filmwallas believe that three or four Mumbai papers represent the whole country, for the simple reason that we subscribe to only these. On a five–six town tour, it came as a revelation to me that every town in the country has its own media and it's far superior to the Mumbai media. I don't think it's necessarily because there are better journalists but, rather, it's because of the relatively less polluted atmosphere.

On the brighter side, I don't think either we film folk or the media are all that bad because after all the pressures and the frustrations we go through, we are at least entertaining people, each in our own way. Whether it's a lie or a truth or half-lie, what is the big deal? If the common man is interested in knowing who slept with whom and who slapped whom, the media will supply the information, and we film industry folk will supply it to the media. I think it's a fantastic threesome.

I want to sum up this chapter by taking the line from *Company* which best describes both people in the film industry and the media, '*Yeh bas hamare dhande ki jaat hai.*'

Chapter 32

The 'Inbetweenists'

WHAT I'VE REALIZED OVER the years is that are people who do and people who don't want to do, but the majority of the people can't decide what to do. I call them the inbetweenists, because they are neither successful in their individual achievements nor are they failures who have at least tried to become successful. They have such very clear opinions on what I should be doing and what I should not be doing, but when I ask them what they're doing themselves, they go blank. They also have an opinion on everything that's happening in the world, and defend their opinion with seemingly unshakeable conviction. This breed of people you can also meet in the comments section of my blog.

These inbetweenists are the kind of people who talk about

why America should or should not have gone to war with Iraq, why a certain cricket player should not have hit a certain ball, why a film should not have been made in a certain way, etc.

The amazing thing about the inbetweenists is that they can jump to a diametrically opposite position so very rapidly, depending on the outcome of an act. For instance, I remember sitting with some distributors who were about to release the remake of a superhit Marathi film, *Maherchi Sadi*, called *Saajan Ka Ghar* in Hindi. They were describing a scene in the original film where this guy is tied a rakhee by his step-sister, who everybody in the family thinks is bad luck for them. Later, he meets with an accident and loses his hand. When everyone starts blaming her for the tragedy, the guy raises the hand with the rakhee and says it's the rakhee which saved one hand at least. The distributors ecstatically told me that this one scene was enough to make the cash registers ring across the country. The film bombed, and a few days later I was with the same group where some guy was telling them they must have been mad to invest in a film which had scenes as stupidly melodramatic as the rakhee scene. They keep quiet as they could not argue with the fact that the film had failed. A few days later, I overheard the same group ripping apart the filmmaker for putting such stupidly melodramatic scenes in the film.

Another instance is when first-time director Shankar was making a film called *Gentleman*, which was based on the subject of capitation fee. The entire south industry wrote it off before the release, saying that capitation fee was too limited a subject to be made into a commercial film. When the film broke all box office records, the same people said that capitation fee was a subject of universal interest. Now the Hindi rights were purchased and the film was made, starring Chiranjeevi and directed by Mahesh Bhatt. There was much anticipation of its mega success based on its performance in the south. The film bombed and the unanimous feedback was that capitation fee was too trivial a subject to be made into a commercial film!

When a well-known filmmaker saw *Satya* before its release, he told me that the background music was too loud and melodramatic, and also that nobody would want to see bearded sweaty faces. When I met him at a party a few months later, after the film had become a cult hit, he told me that there was a lot of appreciation for the background score and that it was largely responsible for *Satya*'s universal success, otherwise it would have remained a niche or so-called art film. He also said the realistic faces were a welcome change from the conventional chocolaty Bollywood faces.

With all the instances I am talking about, the point I am trying to make is that the inbetweenists keep rapidly changing their opinions before, during and after the fact with equal conviction. The reason for this is two-fold. One is that they in the first place have to have an opinion on everything as they don't want to feel dumb and incapable of predicting success or failure, and two is that they don't want to be caught on the wrong side of success if their predictions go wrong. So they always have a theory ready, if their predictions do go wrong. Their conviction also comes from a very primitive sense of self-righteousness. They consider themselves the representatives of the good and just and their belief systems, however tenuous, are strangely even stronger than those of the people who succeed and also the people who fail in trying to succeed. The inbetweenists invariably hate anybody who questions their values, which makes them spew venom against anyone who does so.

They keep waiting for the man who is climbing up the ladder to fall down, so that his falling makes them feel as if they have risen. They just stand at the bottom of the ladder and keep commenting on the climber. The only thing they can ever look forward to is for the climber to fall down.

Another thing about the inbetweenists is that they themselves don't realize that they are inbetweenists. This is because their very life force depends on their convincing themselves of whatever they are convinced about for that moment. Their convictions change with time and situations, but in the end the inbetweenists do not really matter in the scheme of things as they will never ever have that one conviction in their lives that makes one a doer, which is to take even one step up the ladder.

I, for one, am very glad that a vast majority of the people in the world are inbetweenists for the simple reason that there is then that much less competition on the ladder!

Chapter 33

The Day I Toppled the Maharashtra Chief Minister

THERE WERE REPORTS IN the media that I was planning a film on the 26/11 terrorist incident that shook Mumbai and India, and since I was casting Riteish Deshmukh in it, his dad Mr Vilasrao Deshmukh invited me to visit the site—which understandably created widespread outrage.

These reports were completely false.

What happened was this:

I have known Riteish for years, as I have done films with him and also since we belong to the same fraternity. On that day, I went to meet Riteish to discuss *Rann,* my new film with him, which incidentally has nothing to do with terrorism. As we were talking, Riteish said that his dad was going to the Taj and he wanted to go with him. So since I was with him, I accompanied him there. Mr Vilasrao had never been formally introduced to me, and he didn't even know that I was with Riteish, as Riteish and I were in another car.

As far as Riteish is concerned, his information was that the areas we would be able to see were the ones where investigations had already been completed.

By the time we reached the Taj, there were more than sixty-seventy people there including police officers, bureaucrats and hotel staff. In that whole crowd, I doubt Mr Vilasrao even noticed me.

Yes, an amazing coincidence gave me the opportunity of seeing the site of the carnage, and I would like to know how many people would have passed it up?

Now my question is, what is it that could have been affected by my being there? If the officers thought that it would amount to a breach of security or I would see things which I was not supposed to, they would have stopped me. And if they had stopped me, why the hell would Mr Vilasrao have forced them to let me in? The reason they did not stop me was simply that the areas we were shown were those where investigations had already been completed and footage of which had already been shown thousands of times on TV. In fact, I saw far less there than I had already seen on TV. So why did my seeing broken glass, upturned tables and bullet-riddled walls, which the whole country had seen a thousand times on TV, create an outrage? Here's why.

After seeing the footage which ironically was shot by Mr Vilasrao's own team and given to the TV channels, media minds started speculating about my presence there and developed conspiracy theories, and to support their speculation they used slow motion techniques, putting a red circle around me and flickering arrow marks pointing at me. Add to this voiceovers of their interpretation of why I was there and why Mr Vilasrao took me there, and you have the story which resulted in the understandable outrage.

Even assuming for a moment I went there to research for a film I was planning, what possible information could I have gained as a filmmaker, considering that I had already seen much more on TV? Visiting crime scenes cannot generate research for a film for me, as I am not a forensic scientist. Only one-on-one conversations with investigating officers after they had completed their investigations could have given me the kind of information I would need for a film. Some news channels even suggested that we were disturbing a crime scene. If that was the case, it was a serious lapse of duty on the part of the investigating officers. They didn't stop us because, like I said, they were only showing us areas where investigations had been completed.

I find it shocking that in the wake of such a terrible incident, the media could waste so much telecast time on such inanity, while their job was clearly to debate much more serious issues thrown up by the incident, like national safety and security.

The media likes to portray itself as the sole champion of people's rights in the country, and this makes people believe in it blindly. This is a classic example of the blind leading the blind. The outcome of this can often be ridiculous. If, as some media reports suggested, this episode can even remotely affect the government's standing, I find that almost as dangerous as terrorism.

If people who attack the unarmed are defined as terrorists, then the media at various levels with its coercive methods and insinuations resorts to very similar tactics. A terrorist attacks the mind with fear and kills the body with weapons, the media attacks the mind with its interpretations and kills a person's spirit with its insinuations. In a way, I would say that the media is more dangerous than terrorists because it attacks under the guise of safeguarding values.